Mesopotamia and Iran in the Persian Period: Conquest and Imperialism 539-331 BC

Proceedings of a Seminar in memory of Vladimir G. Lukonin

Funded by a gift from
Raymond and Beverly Sackler

Edited by John Curtis

THE BRITISH MUSEUM PRESS

© 1997 The Trustees of the British Museum

Published in 1997 by British Museum Press
A division of the British Museum Company Ltd
38 Russell Square, London WC1B 3QQ

Reprinted 2005

A catalogue record for this book is available
from the British Library

ISBN-10:   0-7141-1142-2
ISBN-13:   978-0-7141-1142-1

Designed and typeset by Andrew Shoolbred
Printed and bound in Great Britain by Henry Ling Ltd.

Front jacket: The Cyrus Cylinder. This records in
Babylonian cuneiform Cyrus' conquest of Babylon
in 539 BC and describes how he restored the worship
of Marduk and returned to their homes the gods and
peoples deported by the Late Babylonian kings.

Back jacket: Stone relief from Persepolis, *c*.485 BC,
showing a bearded male sphinx wearing a
divine headdress.

Contents

Acknowledgements

Many people have helped in the preparation of this book, and grateful thanks are due to all of them. Bernadette Heaney has put some of the articles and other materials on disk and has been of great assistance with the preliminary editorial work. Lisa Bliss has been responsible for whatever photographic work was needed here in the British Museum, often at very short notice, and Ann Searight has helped with the illustrations, including drawing the map of Iraq and Iran. Last but not least, Carolyn Jones of British Museum Press has again seen this book through the press, as she did its two predecessors, with her usual skill and efficiency.

This publication has been subsidised by a generous gift from Raymond and Beverly Sackler, who not only attended the seminar but have supported the work of the Department of Western Asiatic Antiquities in many other ways. Their help and encouragement is much appreciated.

List of Illustrations

Preface

by John Curtis

In this volume are published the proceedings of the third Lukonin Memorial Seminar which was devoted to 'Relations between Mesopotamia and Iran in the Achaemenid Period'. It was held at the British Museum on 18 July 1995. During the course of the day there were five lectures (Fig. 1), following an introduction by J.E. Curtis (British Museum). First, C.B.F. Walker (British Museum) spoke about 'Achaemenid Chronology and Babylonian Sources' and E. Haerinck (University of Gent) about 'Babylonia under Achaemenid Rule'. After lunch, there were lectures from R. Boucharlat (French Research Institute in Iran) on 'Susa under Achaemenid Rule', T.C. Mitchell (London) on 'Achaemenid History and the Book of Daniel' and D.B. Stronach (University of California, Berkeley) on 'Achaemenid Archaeology on the Iranian Plateau'. Following the seminar and a reception in the Assyrian Basement, the annual dinner for the Friends of the Ancient Near East took place in the Lion-Hunt Gallery (Figs 2–3).

All lectures are included here, but mostly in a revised form to take account of subsequent comment and also reflecting the fact that there are inevitably differences between oral and written presentations. Two previous seminars, in 1991 and 1993, dealt with relations between Mesopotamia and Iran in earlier periods, and have been published under the titles *Early Mesopotamia and Iran: Contact and Conflict c. 3500–1600 BC* (London 1993) and *Later Mesopotamia and Iran: Tribes and Empires 1600–539 BC* (London 1995). It is sad to have to record here that one of the participants in the Second Lukonin Seminar, Professor Dr Peter Calmeyer, has died since the publication of the volume. He was a likeable and distinguished scholar who made many contributions of fundamental importance to the archaeology and history of Iran and Mesopotamia, particularly in the Achaemenid period. He passed away on 22 November 1995 at the relatively early age of 65 years, and he will be sadly missed. To return to the two previous volumes, this book is intended as a sequel to them, and it is hoped to continue the series in 1997 with a seminar on the Parthian and Sasanian periods.

Since the establishment of the lecture and seminar programme in 1989, there have been lectures and seminars in alternate years. In the inaugural year B.B. Piotrovskii lectured on 'Ancient Iran and the Caucasus'. Then, in 1990, R.H. Dyson spoke on 'Hasanlu and Iron Age Iran', and in 1992 E.O. Negahban talked about 'Marlik and Late Bronze Age Iran'. On 13 July 1994, Dr Prudence Harper (Fig. 4) gave a lecture on 'Persia and the West in the Late Sasanian period'. She examined Sasanian material culture of the sixth–seventh centuries AD, noted parallels in Byzantine and East Roman art and pointed to examples of continuity with the art of ancient Mesopotamia. She showed how the stag and snake contest scene that occurs on a seal of the mid-Sasanian period could be traced back to third millennium BC Mesopotamia, and pointed to iconographic parallels between Lamashtu amulets of early first millennium BC Mesopotamia and the representations of demons on Sasanian period amulets and incantation bowls. Connections between Sasanian art and that of the west were demonstrated by the Roman motif of Romulus and Remus with a wolf, which also appeared in Sasanian art but in modified forms. Western influence could also be detected at Taq-i Bustan, the Sasanian grottoes probably dating from the time of Chosroes II (AD 598–621). For example, there was the possible parallel with a Roman triple-arched victory monument, and the winged figures on the spandrels of the arch were comparable to female Nikes in late Roman art and to angels in early Christian art. At the same time, there were many oriental features such as the hunting scenes on the side walls of the main *iwan*, and the decorative scheme at Taq-i Bustan clearly derived from Neo-Assyrian palaces and Persepolis. The great lion-bird that appeared as a pattern on some of the garments, and occurs also on Sasanian silver and stucco, had connections with the Mesopotamian lion-griffin of the ninth–seventh centuries BC. A related creature could also be found at Parthian Hatra and on a lintel from George Smith's excavations at Nineveh. The rear part of the lion-bird consisted of a peacock tail and peacocks – or at least peacock plumage – also figured prominently in Late Roman and Byzantine art.

As has been explained elsewhere, the Lukonin Memorial Seminars or Lectures at the British Museum came into being as an adjunct to the Lukonin Memorial Fund, now called the Ancient Persia Fund, which is under the auspices of the British Academy. When it was first established, one of the principal aims of the Ancient Persia Fund was to promote interest in Ancient Iran and the lecture or seminar series at the British Museum, suggested and funded by Raymond and Beverly Sackler, has proved to be a most effective way of doing this. Now, Dr and Mrs Sackler have proposed a new initiative which promises to be equally fruitful. This is the Raymond and Beverly Sackler Scholar Programme in Ancient Iranian Studies as a Tribute to Mary Anna Marten. Under the terms of this benefaction, an annual scholarship in Ancient Iranian Studies will be awarded, tenable at the British Museum. Successful applicants will be expected to undertake research in the Department of Western Asiatic Antiquities, and may at the same time be required to do some administrative work and possibly also some teaching. This is a further indication of Raymond and Beverly Sackler's commitment to Ancient Near Eastern Studies and their determination to support important research in this area and to publicise the results. In the same vein, it is gratifying that the publication of this book has been funded by a gift from them. Nor should we forget to mention the Mesopotamian, Anatolian and Egyptian galleries at the British Museum which it has been possible to refurbish with the help of generous donations from the Sacklers. The Sacklers thus continue to earn the gratitude and admiration of Near Eastern scholars all around the world. It would be no exaggeration to say that their generosity is already making a significant difference in a subject that is struggling to achieve the recognition it deserves.

1 *Left* The speakers at the Third Lukonin Memorial Seminar in July 1995. From left: Professor D.B. Stronach; C.B.F. Walker; Professor E. Haerinck; T.C. Mitchell; Dr R. Boucharlat.

2 *Right* Dr Raymond Sackler, flanked by the Hon. Mrs M.A. Marten and Dr P.R.S. Moorey, at the annual dinner for the Friends of the Ancient Near East, July 1995.

3 *Below* Dr Robert Anderson, Director of the British Museum, flanked by Mrs Beverly Sackler (right) and Mrs Linda Noe Laine, at the annual dinner for the Friends of the Ancient Near East, July 1995.

4 *Below right* Dr Prudence O. Harper, who delivered the Lukonin Memorial Lecture in July 1994.

Introduction

by John Curtis

The Achaemenid period is usually regarded as beginning in 550 BC when Cyrus the Great deposed the Median king Astyages and established himself as undisputed king of the Medes and the Persians. Cyrus was now master of lands that had previously been controlled by the Medes. In Anatolia, Cyrus extended that influence to the west of the River Halys by defeating King Croesus of Lydia and capturing Sardis. In the north-east he reached the River Jaxartes (Syr Darya) and may have got even further than this. In 539 BC he turned his attention westwards to Mesopotamia and in that year captured Babylon. In 612 BC the Babylonians had combined with the Medes to overthrow the Assyrian Empire, and they inherited from the Assyrians control of the western part of the Ancient Near East as far as the Mediterranean Sea, including Syria and Palestine. Now, all these lands fell into the hands of Cyrus. As befitted such a distinguished king, Cyrus built for himself a splendid capital city at Pasargadae on the Iranian Plateau and he was buried in a magnificent stone tomb with a gabled roof. Under his son Cambyses (530–522 BC) Egypt was added to the Persian Empire, and under the next established king, Darius (522–486 BC), the Persian Empire reached its greatest extent, stretching from Libya in the west to the River Indus in the east. His reign also saw the start of the Graeco-Persian wars which continued in the reign of Darius' successor Xerxes (486–465 BC). The attempt to overrun mainland Greece eventually ended with Persian defeats at Salamis and Plataea in 480–479 BC. Although much celebrated in the west as a titanic struggle between democracy and despotism, for the Persian kings these wars were probably little more than a struggle with tiresome neighbours on their far-off western border, and they had little impact elsewhere in the Persian Empire or on the building programme of the Achaemenid kings. Thus, in the latter part of his reign, having already built a splendid palace at Susa in south-west Iran, Darius initiated the building programme at Persepolis, near Pasargadae, which was carried on by Xerxes and Artaxerxes I (465–424 BC). The complex of surviving buildings, including the Apadana and the Hall of 100 Columns, make it today one of the most impressive ancient sites in the world. The Persian Empire was eventually overthrown by Alexander the Great who, with his Macedonian army, crossed the Hellespont in 334 BC and inflicted a series of defeats on the Persian forces of Darius III, the last at Gaugamela in Northern Iraq in 331 BC.

In the 200 years of the Achaemenid Empire, the Persian grip on the Ancient Near East was reinforced by a strong and efficient central administration. It is usually Darius who is given the credit for introducing this. He divided the empire into provinces, each under the charge of a provincial governor or satrap, introduced a system of tax assessment, minted coins and improved communications. In this way, political and economic control was established throughout the empire. The influence on the material culture of the conquered regions is less easy to evaluate, but a distinctive Achaemenid style can certainly be recognised in the field of

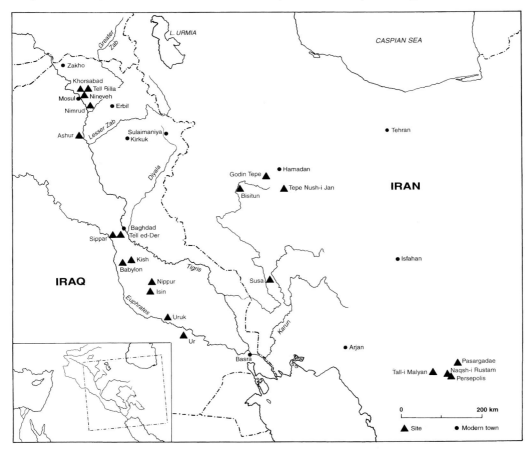

5 Map of Mesopotamia and Iran in the Persian period.

11

arts and crafts. This is particularly the case with luxury goods. Thus, some of the items in the Oxus Treasure, a hoard of gold and silver objects found on the north bank of the River Oxus in what is now Tajikistan, are represented on the Apadana reliefs at Persepolis and were evidently in use at the Persian court at that time. As examples, we might cite the pair of heavy gold bracelets with griffin terminals (Pl. 1) and the silver ibex handle from an amphora. The fact that such items were found on the northern fringes of the empire indicates that they must have been widely distributed. But our concern in this seminar is not with the whole of the Persian Empire, rather with Mesopotamia and with the Iranian heartland itself.

Our intention is to examine these two areas during the Achaemenid period, to consider the connections between them and to assess the influence they had on each other. This subject is of course complex and extensive, and in this book we cannot hope to do more than touch on a few aspects of this interesting question. Christopher Walker sets the background by reviewing the chronology of the period, Ernie Haerinck writes about Babylonia, Rémy Boucharlat describes the great city of Susa in Achaemenid times, and David Stronach writes about early Achaemenid history and sites on the Iranian plateau. Terence Mitchell deals with the Book of Daniel, one of the two Old Testament books which are of particular interest for Achaemenid history. The other is the Book of Esther, which apparently describes a harem intrigue in the latter part of the reign of Xerxes. In this introduction, I will confine myself to drawing attention to some general points and considering a few issues of particular interest to myself.

To start with Iran, it is generally recognised that Iranian art and architecture during the Persian period were eclectic, in that influences, ideas and inspiration were drawn from a large number of sources. Among them are indigenous or native Iranian, Urartian, Ionian, Egyptian, Assyrian and Babylonian. It is the last two that concern us here. To what extent, then, did Achaemenid Iran draw on the Assyro-Babylonian legacy from Mesopotamia to the west?

It is generally accepted that the standard plan for an Achaemenid palace or audience hall, the so-called *apadana*, is Iranian in form if not in inspiration. The developed plan consists of a columned hall with porticoes at the sides and square towers at the corners. Examples of such buildings include Darius' palace at Susa, first excavated by W.K. Loftus in 1850–52 (Curtis 1993), the two palaces at Pasargadae (Fig. 21), and the Apadana itself at Persepolis (Wilber 1969: fig. opp. p. 1). Although the plan of these buildings owes nothing to Mesopotamia, there is, however, clearly some Mesopotamian influence in the decorative scheme. Thus, the colossal winged human-headed bulls, best represented in the Gate of All Nations at Persepolis (Wilber 1969: fig. on p. 11), are clearly copies of their Assyrian counterparts. Then there are the reliefs at Pasargadae in Gate R and in the two palaces. In Gate R there is a winged figure with a fantastic crown (Fig. 17) and in the doorways in Palace S there are the remains of reliefs showing bull-men, fish-cloaked genies and figures with eagles' feet (Fig. 18, Pl. 14). Those in Palace P show the king with an attendant (Col. Pl. VII). As David Stronach himself has written (1978: 295): 'In deference to the role of the Achaemenians as the effective heirs of the once mighty Assyrian kings, Cyrus borrowed the time-honoured guardian symbols of the crumbling palaces of Nimrud, Nineveh, and Khorsabad'. There are also doorway reliefs, generally more elaborate, in a number of the buildings at Persepolis, most notably in the Hall of 100 Columns. Also attested at Persepolis is the use of stone reliefs to decorate long stretches of wall. This technique finds its most famous expression in the celebrated Apadana reliefs. It is hard to resist the conclusion that the idea of decorating palace walls with stone reliefs in Achaemenid Iran came from Assyria, but the style and iconography of these reliefs clearly derive from a range of different sources (Roaf 1983: 96).

And then there is the polychrome glazed brick decoration in Darius' palace at Susa. Particularly well known are the friezes of roaring lions and guardsmen, the so-called 'Immortals', and the panel showing a pair of winged human-headed lions beneath a winged disc (Amiet 1988: figs 80–81, 83). Such panels were usually placed at a high level on courtyard walls. Interestingly, the technique of manufacture of these bricks is different from that of the Assyrian and Babylonian bricks which they superficially resemble. The Achaemenid bricks are made of 'a very coarse quartz faience' as opposed to mud tempered with straw, and also the colours are separated by raised black lines (Dayton 1978: 382–3).[1] In spite of this technological difference, however, there is no doubt that there is a connection, because in an inscription describing the construction of his palace at Susa, Darius says that 'the men who wrought the baked brick, those were Babylonians' (Kent 1953: 144).

How these architectural influences were transmitted to Iran is not entirely clear. In the case of glazed bricks there is no problem because this kind of decoration was widespread in Babylon, including prominent locations such as the Ishtar Gate, and it would have been plainly visible, as well as being very impressive, to Cyrus and his troops in 539 BC. With Assyrian palaces the situation is less straightforward. They were all destroyed in 612 BC and it is by no means clear to what extent the gateway figures and reliefs would have been visible three-quarters of a century later. When mud-brick buildings with timber and mud roofs are put to the torch, the roofs collapse into the rooms below, filling them with debris, and the tops of the walls, when exposed to the weather, rapidly fall down. In a relatively short time the building is represented by a pile or mound of bricky debris. The deterioration is not always so rapid, however, and I suspect that there was a certain amount still to be seen in the Achaemenid period, at least enough to give the Persians a clear impression of the splendid decorative scheme of Assyrian palaces. If this is correct, it is not necessary to postulate that the Medes became familiar with Assyrian buildings from the late seventh century BC onwards and passed their knowledge on to the Persians, either by word of mouth or through a Median architectural tradition which does not survive.

Apart from architecture, Mesopotamian influence can be found in many other areas of Achaemenid culture. First, and most obviously, there is the borrowing of the cuneiform script to write Old Persian inscriptions. The signs were modified and have different values, but broadly speaking the writing system is the same. And then there are cylinder and stamp seals that were impressed on clay tablets. These of course existed in Iran before the Achaemenid period, but both then and later Mesopotamian influence is unmistakable. Let us take, for example, the famous cylinder seal with an inscription of Darius, showing the king in his chariot hunting lions (Pl. 2). This scene is closely paralleled in Assyrian reliefs, particularly those of king Ashurbanipal (668–627 BC) in the North Palace at Nineveh. Mesopotamian influence is also evident in the arts and crafts. For example, there is the fine series of silver bowls with embossed lotus flower decoration and flared rims. There are two bowls of this type in the British Museum. One of them is uninscribed and was found near Erzincan in eastern Turkey in the last century. It was formerly in the Franks Collection (Dalton 1964: no. 180, pl. XXIII). Another has been recently acquired with the help of the National Art Collections Fund (Pl. 3; Curtis, Cowell and Walker 1995). It has an inscription of Artaxerxes I (465–425 BC) and is one of four similar examples that were found some time before 1935, possibly in Hamadan.[2] As was recognised long ago by Heinz Luschey (1939), such bowls are a development from the classic Assyrian carinated bowl.

These Mesopotamian influences on Iranian culture, however, all derive from the halcyon days before Mesopotamia became part of the Achaemenid empire. After that, it was a subject area and indigenous Mesopotamian culture, while not moribund, did not flourish as before. A new world order had arrived, and economic and cultural influences, following close on the heels of political power, were flooding from east to west and not vice versa.

In Iran, then, the Achaemenid period was a time of splendour and prosperity. But what of Iraq or Mesopotamia, which is of equal concern to us in this seminar? In fact, after the prosperity of the Late Assyrian and the Late Babylonian periods, the fortunes of Mesopotamia were at a low ebb. The reasons for this state of affairs have been much discussed, and amongst the reasons put forward are punitive taxation and new lines of communication such as the Royal Road bypassing Mesopotamia (Roux 1964: 343–4). Nevertheless, the rich agricultural resources of Babylonia and its potential for producing grain ensured that this area at least was far from destitute. Business transactions are detailed in cuneiform tablets, particularly archives from Babylon and Sippar. Archaeological remains are more elusive. They are attested principally at Babylon, Nippur, Kish, Isin, Uruk, Ur, and Tell ed-Der (Moorey 1980a: 131; Kuhrt 1988: 119; Simpson 1995: 142). This material evidence from Babylonia will be described below in the chapter by Dr E. Haerinck.

It remains for us here, then, to say something about Assyria. After the collapse of Assyria in 612 BC, the history of Northern Iraq is shrouded in obscurity and we do not really know what happened. It is even unclear which of the two victorious powers, the Medes or the Babylonians, now controlled the area. A few years ago I argued (1989: 52–4) that the probable boundary between the two spheres of influence ran along the Lesser Zab and up the River Tigris, with the Babylonians controlling the area to the south and west and the Medes the area to the north and east, and at the moment I see no cogent reasons for changing this view.[3] This would mean that most of the Assyrian 'heartland' was, for some of the time at least, nominally under Median control.[4] However that may be, historical records for this period are practically non-existent and the lack of information about Assyria continues into the Achaemenid period.

In contrast to Babylonia, Assyria seems to have been relatively impoverished in the Persian period. At the former great capitals of Assyria traces of Achaemenid occupation are hard to find,[5] and although some sites are known to have been occupied in the post-Assyrian, Hellenistic and Parthian periods (Dalley 1993), it cannot necessarily be assumed that there was occupation in the intervening Achaemenid period. Nevertheless, there is usually some indication of an Achaemenid presence, however meagre.

Thus at Nimrud, there is post-Assyrian occupation that might extend into the Achaemenid period in various places, including TW53, the Burnt Palace, the Nabu Temple and the South-East Palace (Postgate and Reade 1977–80: 322). This is most marked in the area of the South-East Palace (AB) to the south of the Nabu Temple, where there was also a good deal of Hellenistic occupation. Some of the pottery from here has been identified as Achaemenid (Oates and Oates 1958: 119, pl. XXVIII/13–14; Mallowan 1966: I, 298–9, fig. 277). In the Burnt Palace, evidence was found for a workshop producing opaque red glass, which D. Barag dates to the Achaemenid period (Barag 1985: 59). In the South-West Palace at Nimrud, W.K. Loftus found a bronze strainer of Achaemenid date (Moorey 1980b: 186, pl. Ia) apparently together with an eye-of-Horus amulet from the same place. The drawing by Loftus' artist, William Boutcher, is reproduced here (Pl. 4).[6] Lastly, it is possible that a large post-Assyrian building in the area of the Central Palace could also be Achaemenid.[7]

At Ashur, a few of the graves can be dated to the Achaemenid period on the basis of their contents (e.g. graves 715, 811, Haller 1954: 71, fig. 88, pl. 16d), and it is not impossible that the celebrated hoard of silver jewellery, found in a jar in room 63 of the New Palace (Guillini *et al.* 1985: nos. 214–21), may be of Achaemenid date. The two silver bracelets with lotus flower terminals are similar to an example found far away at al Mina on the Mediterranean coast in Syria. This bracelet comes from a level dated by Woolley to *c.* 520–430 BC (Woolley 1938: 145, 167, fig. 23).

At Khorsabad, the erstwhile capital of Sargon, there are also traces of Achaemenid occupation. Thus, some of the objects found in post-Assyrian levels in the Nabu Temple appear to be Achaemenid. For example, there are two silver bracelets with ram's head terminals and a silver earring (Loud and Altman 1938: pls 59/123, 127, 60/166).

For Nineveh itself, it would be surprising if a thorough review of the evidence on the ground and the scattered archaeological material did not reveal some indication of Achaemenid occupation, but such a study has not yet been undertaken.

This apparent poverty in Northern Iraq accords well with the observations of the Greek general Xenephon, who with the 'Ten Thousand' Greek mercenaries marched through this area in 401 BC, following the defeat at Cunaxa of Cyrus the Younger whom they had come to help. In his *Anabasis* Xenephon describes Nimrud, which he calls Larissa, as being deserted, but he says that 'many of the natives from the neighbouring villages'[8] had taken refuge on the ziggurat (III.4.7–9). From there, a day's march brought them to the city of Mespila (which name has been plausibly identified with Mosul), which is described as 'a large undefended fortification'. There is no doubt that the fortification itself was Nineveh, as the walls are described quite exactly, having a foundation of polished stone 'in which there were many shells', which was 50 feet high and surmounted by a brick wall 100 feet high (III.4.10–11).

From Nineveh the army turned to the north-west, keeping to the east side of the River Tigris. After about five days of marching 'they noticed a kind of palace with a number of villages in its neighbourhood'. To get to these villages, they first had to fight their way through some hilly or mountainous country, but it was worth the effort. They found 'plenty of food – wheat-flour and wine and a lot of barley that had been stored there for horses. All this had been collected for the man who was satrap of the country' (III.4.24–31). It would obviously be of great interest to know where this satrap's palace was. If Xenephon's account is to be believed, it must have been an important Achaemenid-period settlement. Unfortunately, however, there are no known ancient sites that are obvious candidates. Layard, whose knowledge of the geography of this area is practically unsurpassed, believed that at this stage in their journey the Greeks must have been near modern Zakho (Layard 1853: 61, and map of Assyria opp. p. 686), so the important Achaemenid site should probably be sought in its vicinity.[9]

A major difficulty in the quest for Achaemenid sites, however, is that we still cannot identify with any degree of confidence Achaemenid pottery in Northern Iraq. In this connection, the recent publication of the pottery from the first millennium BC levels at Kharabeh Shattani, a small site in the Eski Mosul Dam Salvage Project, is very welcome. In the report it is argued (Goodwin 1995; Simpson 1995) that the pottery dates from the Achaemenid period, but although the case is quite convincing it is not yet conclusively proven.

Surprisingly, if we are interpreting the evidence correctly, Northern Iraq enjoyed greater prosperity in the following Hellenistic period, ushered in after Alexander defeated Darius III at Gaugamela in 331 BC. There was apparently more land now under cultivation, and an increase in the number of village settlements. Yet Mesopotamia's gain was Iran's loss. As we have described, the Achaemenid period ended when Alexander marched into Iran, looted Susa and burnt Persepolis. The city was badly damaged by this act of wanton destruction, but Persepolis remains today a grand and evocative site, the symbol of an era and a civilisation which is still not properly understood or evaluated in the west.

Notes

1 See Harper *et al.* 1992: 223–4; Moorey 1994: 319.

2 Others are in the Metropolitan Museum of Art, the Freer Gallery, and the Reza Abbasi collection in Tehran.

3 *Pace* Kuhrt 1995: 243, 251.

4 In the inscribed clay barrel known as the Cyrus Cylinder, which was found at Babylon, Cyrus describes how after his conquest of Babylon images (of the gods) were restored to various shrines including, some commentators believe, Nineveh. This has encouraged the view that prior to this time neither Cyrus nor the Medes before him controlled Nineveh, but the text is broken at this point and the word Nineveh is restored. In fact, my colleague Irving Finkel will shortly publish a note arguing that it is impossible to restore

'Nineveh' in the gap. The argument is therefore invalidated.

5 For information about other possible Achaemenid period sites in Assyria, see Moorey 1980a: 131; Simpson 1990: 129–31; Kuhrt 1995; and Simpson 1995: 142–3.

6 Also reproduced in Curtis 1983: pl. VIII.

7 Personal communication J.E. Reade.

8 Quotations are taken from the translation of Rex Warner published by Penguin Books (*The Persian Expedition*).

9 An interesting article has recently appeared on the itinerary of the Ten Thousand in Mesopotamia (Joannès 1995), but the author does not discuss the route taken between Mosul and Cizre.

Achaemenid Chronology and the Babylonian Sources

by Christopher Walker

BRITISH MUSEUM

Babylonian and Achaemenid chronology according to Ptolemy

Prior to the discovery and interpretation of the Mesopotamian cuneiform inscriptions the fundamental source for the chronology, both relative and absolute, of the later Babylonian and Achaemenid kings (747–324 BC) was the king-list known as *Canon Basileon*, compiled by the astronomer Claudius Ptolemaeus (Ptolemy) of Alexandria (*fl. c.* AD 130–175) perhaps borrowing from the work of earlier astronomers of Alexandria. It was published in his *Handy Tables*, and survives in a considerably augmented form in Byzantine versions of Theon of Alexandria's revision of the *Handy Tables*. The most recent edition is by G. J. Toomer (1984: 9–12).

Ptolemy's *Canon* was compiled for astronomical purposes, to achieve consistency in citing and manipulating original astronomical data. So it deliberately uses two chronological conventions: the Egyptian year of 365 days and the era of Nabonassar (Babylonian Nabu-naṣir). The first year of each king's reign was assumed to begin on the first day of the month Thoth preceding the actual date of the king's accession. In the case of Nabonassar whose first full regnal year began in the spring of 747 BC, Ptolemy's scheme equates to a beginning of his reign on 26 February 747 BC.[1]

In his great astronomical treatise, the *Almagest*, Ptolemy explains that he uses the era of Nabonassar, 'For that is the era beginning from which the ancient observations are, on the whole, preserved down to our time' (*Almagest* III 7; Toomer 1984: 166). This corresponds with the fact that the earliest surviving Neo-Babylonian astronomical record apparently refers to the accession year of Nabu-naṣir.[2] This text records four lunar eclipses actually observed in the years 747–746 BC. It is in fact the first record of consecutive astronomical phenomena available to us after the so-called 'Venus Tablet of Ammiṣaduqa' some 900 or more years earlier. This large time gap may reflect nothing more than the accidents of preservation and discovery. But it may be that the occasion of observing four lunar eclipses at successive six-monthly intervals beginning immediately after the accession of Nabu-naṣir was what triggered the beginning of the extensive astronomical record-keeping, evidenced by the Diaries (Sachs and Hunger 1988–96), which continued for the next seven centuries at least. 'Diaries' is the term now universally used for the regular series of Babylonian observational records. It may also be this series of astronomical records, rather than more general historical records, which is referred to in the curious story told by Berossus: 'Nabonasaros collected together and destroyed the records of the kings before him in order that the list of the Chaldaean kings might begin with him' (Burstein 1978: 22).

Ptolemy uses in the *Almagest* ten different Babylonian lunar eclipse records, covering the time-span 721–382 BC (Toomer 1984: 685, under 'eclipses, lunar, observations of'). However he records that his predecessor Hipparchus (*fl. c.* 150–125 BC) had also made use of Babylonian lunar eclipse observations and had described them as being 'from the series brought over from Babylon' (Toomer 1984: 211). These include the only eclipse record cited by Ptolemy for which we have an equivalent record surviving from Babylonia, the lunar eclipse of 16 July 523 BC (14/iv/7 Cambyses; Strassmaier 1890: no. 400); it is at first sight embarrassing that in this case Ptolemy gives (according to modern calculation) an inaccurate time for the eclipse and the Babylonians an inaccurate estimate of the eclipse magnitude, but the Cambyses text is now understood to contain a series of predictions rather than observations.[3]

Ptolemy's *Canon* was an artificial scheme designed to provide astronomers with a consistent chronology into which astronomical observation records might be fitted, not to provide historians with a precise record of the accession and death of kings. Nevertheless it has served as the backbone of the chronology of the Neo-Babylonian and Achaemenid periods, and served reliably. Re-adjusted to the Julian calendar, allowing for Ptolemy's assumptions, and taking account of two short periods of confusion which Ptolemy describes as ἀβασίλευτα ('having no king') and of the inclusion in Babylonian king-lists of certain short-lived usurpers, there is no difficulty in correlating Ptolemy's chronology with the vast accumulation of data now available from cuneiform sources. The explanation must lie in the nature of the data to which he had access. Whereas it is clear that many aspects and details of Babylonian mathematical astronomy of the Seleucid period became available to their Greek contemporaries and successors, for example the sexagesimal system, the division of the zodiac into 360 units, the mean values of various periodic phenomena, and the precise workings of the Babylonian lunar System B (for the latter see Neugebauer 1988), the only observational data which appear to have been transmitted relate to lunar eclipses. Moreover, despite the wealth of observational data (including eclipse reports) available to us from Seleucid Babylonia, which should in principle have been easily transmittable to the Greeks, neither Hipparchus nor Ptolemy is recorded as using any Babylonian data later than 382 BC. The later observations which they use were made either in Alexandria or (by Hipparchus) on Rhodes.

The Babylonian astronomical sources

It may be more than coincidence that there is a surviving source which in a single format could have provided Hipparchus and Ptolemy with all the accurate observations and chronology which they needed: the Babylonian eclipse lists. With the exception of one tablet more recently identified (BM 71537; see below) the relevant sources were already published or listed by the late A. Sachs in 1955,[4] under the broad heading 'Planetary and lunar observations, etc.: Moon'. Some of the texts are effectively astronomical Diaries for a single day;[5] others are evidently excerpted from the Diaries, and list (often describing in detail) all observed lunar and solar eclipses within the period which they individually cover, together with the dates (and often times) of eclipse 'possibilities' (i.e. eclipses not observable at Babylon because they took place wholly when the moon was below the horizon or during the hours of daylight, or eclipses which did not occur at all because the luni-solar conjunction or opposition was insufficiently close). The possibility of a lunar (or solar) eclipse occurs at intervals of six, or sometimes five, months, and this principle and the patterns of six- or five-month intervals were well understood by the Babylonians already by the eighth century BC. Solar eclipses may occur at half a month's interval before or after a lunar eclipse, but the pattern of six- or five-month intervals differs from lunar eclipses (hence lunar and solar eclipse lists are easily distinguishable). In principle a solar eclipse may occur both before and after a lunar eclipse, but this was not recognised by the Babylonians who only allowed one solar eclipse possibility at each luni-solar conjunction.

Some of the eclipse lists give the data in a conventional list format in one or more columns,[6] whereas others make use of the fact that eclipses of the same character typically recur at intervals of eighteen years (or more precisely 223 lunar months), the so-called Saros period, to construct elaborate tables setting out all the thirty-eight eclipse possibilities within each eighteen-year cycle in parallel columns, with the five-month intervals specified and often with rulings between each eclipse possibility.[7] Although many of the texts are poorly written and may represent little more than rough notes or memoranda, some of the tablets are beautifully written archival or library copies, in one case (Sachs *et al.* 1955: no. 1413) with 'firing holes' such as are found at an earlier period among the Assyrian tablets of Ashurbanipal's library at Nineveh (seventh century BC).

Two of the tablets formatted in Saros cycles are theoretical texts, setting out the pattern of eclipse possibilities with the dates given in terms of regnal year and lunar month, and with the position of the five-month interval carefully marked, but without any statement of whether an eclipse had been observed. These are the so-called 'Saros Canon' and the 'Solar Saros', both written in the Seleucid period.[8]

Among the remaining tablets formatted in Saros cycles one group stands out: Sachs *et al.* 1955: nos. 1414, 1415+ and 1419. They appear to be part of a set prepared by a single scribe for official purposes, describing a total of twenty-four Saros cycles covering the period (probably) from 747 to 315 BC. Horizontal rulings separate successive eclipse possibilities and vertical rulings separate the eclipse cycles (see Figs 6-7). Unusually these tablets turn not from top to bottom but sideways. Each tablet had part of twelve Saros cycles on the obverse and part of twelve more on the reverse. The complete Saros cycle of thirty-eight eclipses (or possibilities) was divided up into segments and written on (probably) eight tablets, of which we have fragments of three. If the series be deemed to start with the first eclipse of the reign of Nabonassar (which is not yet proven) then the surviving fragment of Sachs *et al.* 1955: no. 1414 dealt with (at least) eclipses 34 and 35 of the cycle, Sachs *et al.* 1955: no. 1415+ dealt with (at least) eclipses 16–20, and Sachs *et al.* 1955: no. 1419 dealt with (at least) eclipses 26–28. In all probability each tablet dealt with five eclipses, with a final tablet covering eclipses 36–38.[9] The

6-7 The lunar eclipse table fragment BM 32234 (Sachs *et al.* 1955: no. 1419). Parts of five columns survive on each side. The numbering of the columns reflects the proposed overall scheme of 24 cycles. The eclipse possibilities are identified by month and year of the Babylonian or Achaemenid king and by day, month and year in the Julian calendar. Each column is eighteen years later than the previous column, and reading down the columns each eclipse possibility is six months later than the previous possibility.

Obverse				
viii	ix	x	xi	xii
[...]	22/iii/591 BC	2/iv/573 BC	13/iv/555 BC	23/iv/537 BC
[...]	xii/13 Nebuchadnezzar II	xii/31 Nebuchadnezzar II	i/1 Nabonidus	ii/2 Cyrus
4/ix/609 BC	15/ix/591 BC	25/ix/573 BC	6/x/555 BC	17/x/537 BC
vi/17 Nabopolassar	vi/14 Neb II	vi/32 Neb II	vii/1 Nabonidus	vii/2 Cyrus
[...]	12/iii/590 BC	22/iii/572 BC	3/iv/554 BC	[...]
[...]	xii/14 Neb II	xii/32 Neb II	xiib/1 Nabonidus	[...]

Reverse				
xiii	xiv	xv	xvi	xvii
[...]	[...]	[...]	5/vi/465 BC	[...]
[...]	[...]	[...]	iii/21 Xerxes	[...]
28/x/519 BC	7/xi/501 BC	19/xi/483 BC	29/xi/465 BC	11/xii/447 BC
vii/3 Darius I	viii/21 Darius I	viii/3 Xerxes	viii/21 Xerxes	ix/18 Artaxerxes II

chronological range of the series is proven by Sachs *et al.* 1955: no. 1414; although it is only the bottom left-hand corner of a tablet, its first preserved eclipse possibility (eclipse 35) is datable to 9 April 731 BC (in year 1 of Ukin-zer) and its last to 13 December 317 BC (in year 7 of Philip Arrhidaeus). While it would be presumptuous to suggest that these tablets represent Hipparchus' and Ptolemy's original Babylonian source, their source must have been something similar.

Two other features of this particular series of tablets are of interest. The times of eclipses are given, and, on each occasion in the preserved text where it is noted that an eclipse was not observed at Babylon, a precise time is given for the luni-solar opposition (syzygy); in many cases this time corresponds closely to the time of an eclipse observable elsewhere on the earth's surface. The earliest attested predictions appear to be rounded (perhaps to the nearest hour); nevertheless we appear to be dealing with a surprisingly sophisticated eclipse theory already in the eighth or seventh century BC (Stephenson and Steele, forthcoming).

In addition the tablets apparently gave details, at the appropriate points, of the death of the reigning king. Such details are a useful supplement to the deductions which one can make from changes in the dating of contemporary economic texts.[10] Only one such reference is preserved in this series of lunar eclipse tables (but see also below on the solar eclipse text BM 71537), but curiously, apart from a single brief citation (A. Sachs quoted in Parker and Dubberstein 1956: 17),[11] it remains unpublished. It concerns the death of Xerxes, shortly after a partial lunar eclipse which can be dated to 5 June 465 BC (corresponding to the third month of Xerxes' year 21):

> BM 32234 (Sachs *et al.* 1955: no. 1419) Rev. col. xvi
> (the beginning of the eclipse report is lost)
> *ina* ⌈18?⌉ [...]
> 40? GAR Í[R *u* ZALÁG] ⌈TÚG⌉ AN ⌈GAR⌉
> *ina* KI 4-ÁM *ár šá* PA *ád* KIN DIR
> IZI 1⌈4?⌉ ⌈*hi?*- *ši?*⌉-*ár-šú* DUMU-*šú* GAZ-*šú*

'... in 18° [...]; 40° (duration) of onset, to[tality and clearing up], the "garment of the sky" was present; (the moon) was eclipsed in the area of the rear group of four stars of Sagittarius. (There was an) intercalary month Ulul. On the fourteenth(?) day of the month Ab, Xerxes – his son murdered him.'

Similar features appear in the only known example of a text detailing observed and possible solar eclipses in Saros cycles, BM 71537. Here too horizontal rulings separate successive eclipse possibilities and vertical rulings separate the eclipse cycles, but this tablet turns from top to bottom and the columns continue directly from obverse to reverse. Given the relative infrequency of observed solar eclipses, the small script employed and the very compressed format of this particular tablet, it seems possible that the entire eighteen-year cycle is contained on a single tablet. It is also possible that with twelve eclipse cycles on each side the tablet might have covered the time-span from Nabonassar to Philip in the same manner as

Sachs *et al.* 1955: nos. 1414, etc., do for lunar eclipses. However this suggestion should be taken with considerable caution since at present the earliest solar eclipse recorded in an astronomical Diary is that of 11 April 369 BC, and it is inevitable, given the relative infrequency of visible solar eclipses at any particular location, that solar theory developed later than lunar theory. The tablet contains predictions of solar eclipse times (Steele, forthcoming) and two dates for changes of royal rule, neither of which is directly associated with an observed eclipse:

(1) Obv. col. ii′ line 1′, the last line of an incomplete entry which, to judge by the tabulation, relates to an eclipse possibility on 15 November 359 BC (the month Ab of Artaxerxes II year 46, reads: [... *ina* AŠ.T]E TUŠ-*a*[*b*], '[...] sat [on the thro]ne'. The reference must be to the accession of Artaxerxes III, which followed within six months of the eclipse possibility.

(2) Rev. col. iii′ lines 8–10, a complete entry recording an eclipse possibility which 'passed by' on the 29th of the month Du'uzu in year 21 (of Artaxerxes III) (= 26 July 338 BC), followed by: KIN ¹*ú-ma-kuš* NAM.ME *ár-šú* DUMU-*šú ina* AŠ.TE TUŠ-*ab*, 'Month Ulul, Umakuš (went to his) fate; his son Aršu sat on the throne.' Umakuš here is a Babylonian rendering of Artaxerxes III's throne name usually rendered in Greek as Ochus. 'Went to his fate' is a common Babylonian expression for death, and by contrast with the reference to the death of Xerxes presumably indicates that Artaxerxes III died from natural causes.

These three references on BM 32234 and BM 71537 serve to underline the link seen in antiquity between eclipses and the death of kings; indeed such links underpin the survival of astrology as a significant Mesopotamian contribution to western ideas until at least the seventeenth century AD.

It should be added that the pattern of the eclipse tables is matched by fragments of similar tables of observations of Venus and Jupiter. Thus BM 32299 and BM 45674 (Sachs *et al.* 1955: nos. 1387–8) are fragments of a Neo-Babylonian Venus table in eight-year cycles covering at least the years 463–417 BC; and BM 36823 (Sachs *et al.* 1955: no. 1393) is a fragment of a Jupiter table in twelve-year cycles covering at least the years 526–489 BC.

The lunar calendar
The finer details of historical chronology depend on an understanding of local calendars. It has long been widely accepted that we have detailed control of the lunar calendar of the Neo-Babylonian and Achaemenid periods on the basis of the evidence of contemporary economic and astronomical records. The fundamental tables were printed forty years ago (Parker and Dubberstein 1956) and have never been seriously questioned. The principal problem involved is to determine the years in which a thirteenth lunar month, the 'intercalary' month, was added to bring the lunar year back into line with the solar year, and which intercalary month (second Ulul, month 6b, or second Addar, month 12b) was used. The first list of attested intercalary months for the period was published by F. X. Kugler[12] and was updated

on the basis of new material by Parker and Dubberstein (1956: 4–9). A point of particular interest is when the standard nineteen-year cycle of seven intercalations, known as the 'Metonic cycle' after the Greek astronomer Meton who introduced it to the Athenians in the late fifth century BC, was introduced in Babylonia. Historians of Babylonian astronomy have in recent decades come to the conclusion that the cycle was known to the Babylonians by about 500 BC, and indeed have regarded its recognition as one of the significant factors in the early development of mathematical astronomy in the fifth century BC.[13] Prior to this point, although the New Year never shifted far from the spring equinox it is not clear that any mathematical principle of intercalation was applied.

In this regard it is interesting to note how the evidence for intercalation in the royal archives from Persepolis complements the evidence from Babylonia. The Persepolis Fortification Tablets date to the years 13–28 of Darius I (Hallock 1969: 1 and 3), while the Persepolis Treasury Tablets date from year 30 of Darius I to year 7 of Artaxerxes I (Cameron 1948: 32).[14] The following table summarises the available data for this period. The figures for Babylonia include texts dated to the months Ulul and Addar which indicate that a succeeding intercalary month was expected by the use of ITU MN IGI-ú (*maḫrû*), 'first month MN'.

BC	Darius	Month	Persepolis	Babylonia	Babylonian astronomical tables
			Economic texts (numbers only)		
509/508	13	12b	0	4	
506/505	16	12b	1	12	
503/502	19	6b	5	3	Sachs *et al.* 1955: no. 1393
500/499	22	12b	8	5	
498/497	24	12b	7	7	
495/494	27	12b	1	4	
492/491	30	6b	1	0	
490/489	32	12b	1	3	Sachs *et al.* 1955: no. 1422+
487/486	35	12b	0	2	
	Xerxes				
484/483	2	6b	3	0	
482/481	4?	12b	0	1	
479/478	8?	6b	0	1	
476/475	10	12b	0	0	Sachs *et al.* 1955: no. 1422+
474/473	12	12b	2	0	
471/470	15	12b	0	0	Sachs *et al.* 1955: no. 1422+
468/467	18	12b	0	0	Sachs *et al.* 1955: no. 1422+
465/464	21	6b	0	0	Sachs *et al.* 1955: no. 1419
	Artaxerxes I				
463/462	2	12b	0	0	Sachs *et al.* 1955: no. 1387
460/459	5	12b	1	0	Sachs *et al.* 1955: nos. 1422+, 1388

The principle of seven intercalations in nineteen years is observed (there were intercalations previously in the years 514/513 BC and 511/510 BC (years 8 and 11 of Darius I)). The series has to be completed from the astronomical tables just discussed, but these tables do not conflict with the available economic texts. Most interestingly, the pattern of intercalations is the same at Persepolis as in Babylonia. One wonders how this was achieved. Did Babylonian astronomers advise or instruct the Persian court? Or if the 'Metonic cycle' really had its genesis in this period, did Darius himself have a hand in its origin? It is not difficult to imagine the man who won an empire for himself and ordered the invention of a new cuneiform script for the Persian language instructing his scholars, 'Give me a calendar'. But such speculation may be too fanciful, and the astronomical argument probably stands on firmer ground.

It must be admitted, however, that there are still a few problems with the list of intercalary months during the later years of the Achaemenid empire. For instance, in the sixteenth year of Darius II (408/407 BC), three sources suggest an intercalary Ulul but one an intercalary Addar; in the sixteenth year of Artaxerxes II, two sources suggest an intercalary Ulul but one an intercalary Addar; and two sources (including a contemporary astronomical Diary) suggest an intercalary Addar in the twentieth year of Artaxerxes II (385/384 BC) whereas two other sources (including the Saros canon) attribute the intercalary month to his twenty-first year. These would be minor problems but for the fact that from the reign of Xerxes onwards the evidence from contemporary economic texts diminishes to a small trickle, and from about 370 BC onwards we are very largely dependent on the evidence of the Saros Canon, which, as was explained above, is in principle an expression of Babylonian eclipse theory of the Seleucid period, not history. Indeed it is clear from the evidence of the confused statements of another Babylonian text (BM 33809, unpublished; see provisionally Frame 1992: 18), apparently attempting to list years in which there was an intercalary Ulul, that at least some Babylonian scribes of the Seleucid period did not have access to accurate information about earlier patterns of intercalation. Thus while the chronology of the later Achaemenid period is not likely to be in doubt at any point by more than a month, more supporting evidence in the form of economic or other texts would be welcome.

The chronology of Alexander III (the Great)

In conclusion we may note the astronomical evidence for the arrival in Babylonia and subsequent death of Alexander, whom Ptolemy lists as the last of the Achaemenid kings, perhaps following later Persian tradition which regards Alexander as the half-brother of Darius III. The evidence shows both the occasional apparent absurdity of Ptolemy's chronological convention if seen in purely historical terms, and the value of even small scraps of astronomical data under the right circumstances.

The astronomical Diary for the year 331/330 BC (Sachs and Hunger 1988–96: I, 176–9, Diary No. -330, BM 36761), which began in Babylonian terms as the fifth regnal year of Darius III, records the victory of Alexander (described as 'the king of the world') over Darius (described only as 'the king') at the Battle of Gaugamela (1 October 331 BC). The date is given in the fragmentary Diary as the 24th of the month, and it followed a total lunar eclipse on the evening of the 13th of the month (20 September). The reverse of the same tablet describes Alexander's subsequent victorious entry into Babylon. Ptolemy's chronology however yields a beginning of the astronomical year 'Alexander year 1' almost a year earlier on 14 November 332 BC.

Alexander's death is recorded on a small scrap of a Diary for the year 323/322 BC (Sachs and Hunger 1988–96: I, 206–7, Diary No. -322, BM 45962, with calendar table on p. 218), in extremely laconic fashion: 29 LUGAL NAM.MEŠ DIR AN [...], 'On the 29th the king died; clouds [...] the sky'. By the conventions of Babylonian astronomical Diaries, observations made during the night (from sunset onwards) are preceded by GE$_6$ 29, 'on the night of the 29th', while the simple 29, 'on the 29th', introduces observations or events during the following hours of daylight. Apart from this historical reference the fragment is datable solely by two references to the precise position of Mercury and general statements about the positions of Mars and Saturn. The date of his death is 11 June 323 BC. This is confirmed by the text Sachs *et al.* 1955: no. 1431, a table of observations of precise time intervals between the respective risings or settings of the sun and moon, which records (in extremely abbreviated terminology) the beginning of the following month already in the terms, 'Year 1 of Philip, month III, (the first day of which was equivalent to the) 30th (day of the preceding month), (the time interval between sunset and moonset was) 13°, (because of) cloud not observed'. Thus the clouds which witnessed Alexander's death precluded observation of the crescent of the new moon on the evening of the same (Julian) day.

Notes

1 For a full table of Julian equivalents to Ptolemy's years see Toomer 1984: 11. Modern calculation, based on the Babylonian astronomical text BM 41985 (Sachs *et al.* 1955: no. 1413), would begin Nabu-naṣir's first year on about 21 February 747 BC. Babylonian astronomical texts are cited in this article by both their British Museum numbers and their publication numbers in Sachs *et al.* 1955.

2 BM 41985 (Sachs *et al.* 1955: no. 1413); edited by Huber (1973).

3 Toomer 1984: 253 and n. 58 (where the problem is noted), and Huber 1973.

4 Sachs *et al.* 1955: nos. 1413–30, 1432, 1435–52.

5 Sachs *et al.* nos. 1437, 1438, 1440–42, 1444–50, 1452.

6 Sachs *et al.* 1955: nos. 1413, 1420, 1421, 1429(?), 1432, 1435+1443+1334, 1436, 1439, 1451. Texts are described here as lists unless it is unequivocally clear that they are formatted in Saros cycles.

7 Sachs *et al.* 1955: nos. 1414, 1415+1416+1417, 1418, 1419, 1422+1423+1424, 1425, 1426(+)1427, 1428, 1430.

8 The names are modern. The texts are BM 34597 (first published as Sachs *et al.* 1955: no. 1428) and

BM 36754 (listed as Sachs *et al.* 1955: no. 1430); both were recently edited with a full explanation of the underlying astronomical principles in Aaboe *et al.* 1991. Fragmentary texts similar to the Saros Canon are Sachs *et al.* 1955: nos. 1322+ and 1425.

9 This analysis, if correct, effectively confirms that the series began with Nabu-naṣir's accession year.

10 See in general Parker and Dubberstein 1956: 10–24. There have been a number of more recent studies of individual problems in the light of new evidence which are not detailed here. For a single example see Stolper 1989: 303–5.

11 Despite Sachs's caution the day number appears to the present writer almost certainly to be 14.

12 Kugler 1909–24: 334–5 and 411–22; note also the evidence on pp. 420–2 for years in which particular intercalary months did not occur.

13 See Walker and Britton 1996: 46 and 52. For a more cautious statement see Neugebauer 1975:I, 354–5.

14 For comments on the intercalary months see Cameron 1948: 34. For Darius I year 30 see his text 1a, and Cameron 1965: 169 and 181–2. For Artaxerxes year 7 see Hallock 1960: 91 and 93.

Babylonia under Achaemenid Rule

by E. Haerinck
University of Gent

Cyrus the Great, the founder of the first Persian empire, annexed Babylonia shortly after the prophet Daniel had read the words ('Mene, Mene, Tekel, Parsin') which mysteriously appeared on the walls of the palace of Bel-šarra-uṣur (Belshazzar of the Bible, Daniel 5: 25–8), son of King Nabonidus, and which indicated that the rule of the Neo-Babylonian monarchs was ended. Nabonidus, the last king of the Neo-Babylonian dynasty, had not been popular either with his people or with the powerful priests of the god Marduk. He had refused to participate in the annual religious ceremonies, an essential part of the life of the city, he had promoted the worship of the moon-god Sin over that of the pre-eminent Babylonian deity Marduk, and had offended the people and priests in many other ways. So, when Cyrus entered the city in the autumn of 539 BC, he was greeted by the people as a liberator rather than as a conqueror. In spring 539 the Persian army had started to move down the Diyala Valley and in August of the same year there was a battle at Opis on the Tigris (Meuleau 1965; Cardascia 1989; Dandamayev 1989). On 10 October Sippar surrendered and Nabonidus fled to Babylon. Two days later the Persian army entered Babylon and Nabonidus was taken prisoner. On 29 October Cyrus himself entered the city. His propaganda machine immediately went to work and Cyrus presented himself as a liberator. To strengthen his claim to kingship, Cyrus 'took the hands of the god Marduk', thus making himself the legitimate ruler of the city, as he tells us in the famous Cyrus Cylinder (Cardascia 1989 : 325; Dandamayev 1989 : 328), written in Babylonian cuneiform and discovered by Hormuzd Rassam in 1879 (Pl. 11). He also sent back to their cities the statues of gods which had been brought to Babylon by Nabonidus. Several Babylonian texts also describe Cyrus as a liberator (Dandamayev 1989 : 328). These are exercises in propaganda intended to picture Cyrus as benevolent. On the other hand, sources such as Berossus, Herodotus and Xenophon give us a rather different picture. From them we learn that the Babylonians resisted Cyrus and that the city was taken only after serious fighting. According to Herodotus (I.188–91) the Persians diverted the Euphrates and took the city by surprise. Xenophon has a similar account (*Cyropaedia* VII.5.7–32,58). However that may be, there is no argument that Cyrus restored the old religious customs, returned the statues of the gods to their proper places and also rejuvenated the economic life of the city. He made Babylon one of the principal capitals of his new empire, an empire which extended from the Mediterranean to the Indus. This mighty city became one of the residences of the Achaemenid kings, each of whom spent several months of the year here. Although there were revolts under later kings of the dynasty (in 522, 520 and 482 BC), there was never a serious confrontation (Cameron 1941; de Liagre Böhl 1962, 1968).

Reconstructions of the history and the socio-economic and religious situations, as well as of daily life in Babylonia, are possible thanks to written sources of various types on the one hand and archaeological evidence on the other.[1] The most famous historical inscription of the Persian kings is undoubtedly the Cyrus Cylinder. The excavators of Babylon also discovered fragments of a copy of the rock-carving on the mountain at Bisitun near Kermanshah with the Babylonian version of the great trilingual inscription of Darius (Seidl 1976). There are in addition numerous clay tablets (e.g. archives from the Egibi and Murashu families) which give important information about many aspects of life, including business transactions, inheritance, loans, and legal matters (Cardascia 1951; Stolper 1985). Another type of written evidence is the records left by the classical authors (Wetzel 1950; Joannès 1995) of which the best known is that of Herodotus of Halicarnassus. This traveller and so-called 'father of history' visited Babylon in *c.* 460 BC (Ravn 1942; Wetzel 1944). His description is of great interest, but has to be treated with some caution.

During the rule of the Achaemenid kings, which lasted slightly more than two centuries, life in Mesopotamia underwent radical change, particularly in administration and in religious and economic life. The population of Babylon, and of Mesopotamia in general, was mixed and multilingual, as is shown by a study of the names of people mentioned in contracts (Cardascia 1951; Dandamayev 1969 ; 1989: 332; 1992). In addition to Babylonians, there were peoples of Iranian, Aramaean, Jewish and Egyptian origin (Zadok 1976). Although Babylonian cuneiform, written on clay tablets, remained in use throughout the period, it was gradually replaced by Aramaic, another semitic language but one with a much less complicated script. It had a relatively simple alphabet instead of the complex cuneiform signs and ideograms, and it could be written on parchment as well as clay. Aramaic soon became the lingua franca of the empire. Babylonia, the ninth satrapy of the Achaemenid empire, was a rich province and was also the most heavily taxed. It had to pay yearly one thousand silver talents (some 30 tons), and also had to support the army and the king for one-third of the year. The greed of the Persian treasury under the later kings had serious consequences for the Babylonian economy. As we learn from numerous clay tablets, prices gradually went up. By the second half of the fifth century BC interest on loans was 40–50 per cent, while some two centuries earlier, during the reign of Nebuchadnezzar II, it had been only 10 per cent (Dubberstein 1939). Almost all south Mesopotamian cities (e.g. Ur, Uruk, Nippur and Kish) continued to be occupied during the Achaemenid period and it was the most flourishing area (Gasche 1995). North Mesopotamia, on the other hand, is less well documented, although archaeology and textual evidence indicate that there were some centres of importance, for example Tell Billa and Erbil (Dandemayev 1987; Kuhrt 1995). Other sites were virtually deserted, for example Ashur and Nimrud, which is confirmed by Xenophon's description in the *Anabasis* (III.4.6–8).

Excavations support Cyrus' claim that he entered Babylon without a struggle: there is no indication of destruction and the city did not really suffer under Persian occupation. Like all Near Eastern cities, Babylon was surrounded by substantial inner and outer walls. It is possible that by the fifth century BC the outer wall had crumbled and fallen down, since Herodotus mentions only one. Nevertheless, this traveller was full of admiration for the beauty, wealth and pomp of Babylon, which also under Persian occupation continued to be a metropolis of exceptional importance. During the Achaemenid period the street plan did not change much, and most houses were still inhabited. The Merkes quarter, however, lost some of its importance, and several houses fell into decay (Reuther 1926: 34, 76, 121–2, 148).

Religion was an important part of Achaemenid politics, and the Persians allowed the inhabitants of conquered regions to continue with their own beliefs. Babylonian temples looked much the same as in the Neo-Babylonian period, and many of the sanctuaries, such as E-sagil, E-ḫursag-tilla, E-maḫ and Temple Z continued in use even in the following Seleucid period. In general, the Achaemenids concentrated on restoring and maintaining religious monuments, but even so some temples decayed, including the E-temen-anki ziggurat, which was described by Herodotus. By the end of the Achaemenid period this structure had become so ruinous that Alexander the Great decided to replace it. Before this could be done a huge mass of baked bricks had to be removed, and this debris was discovered by the German Archaeological Expedition in the Homera mound. While religious toleration was practised by Cyrus and Darius, Darius' son Xerxes punished the Babylonians for their revolt in 482 BC by ordering the removal from Esagila of the golden statue of the national god Marduk (Kuhrt and Sherwin-White 1987; Dandamayev 1993). This meant that the important annual New Year (Akitu) festival, which happened in the spring, could no longer take place. In *c.* 462 BC, however, his successor, Artaxerxes I, allowed the Marduk priests to restart the cult and restored to them their property. In addition to their religious role, the temples in Mesopotamia had always played a major part in political and economic life. They possessed vast landed estates and provided work for thousands of labourers. However, during the Achaemenid period this role was curtailed, and for the first time in their history they were obliged to pay taxes and to accept state control of their financial activities.

Although Babylon was one of the principal capitals of the Achaemenid rulers and their heirs apparent, they do not seem to have built many residences there. Instead, they continued to use the Neo-Babylonian palaces. However, Artaxerxes II ordered the construction of a pavilion or a small palace (previously attributed by us to Darius I) 34.80 m long by 20.50 m

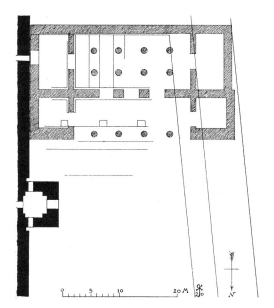

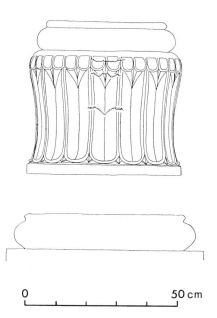

8 Plan of the Achaemenid palace at Babylon.

9 Column bases from the Achaemenid palace at Babylon

wide, in a purely Iranian style, on the Kasr mound, at the west of the Southern Citadel (Koldewey 1931: 120–25, pls 26–8; Wetzel 1931: 15–16, fig. 4; Wetzel *et al.* 1957: 25–7; Klengel 1962; Haerinck 1973; Vallat 1989; Gasche 1991). All the elements indicate its Persian origin, and even minor details show Achaemenid characteristics. Excavation of this building was not easy, because only the foundations remained more or less complete; most of the superstructure had not survived. The plan is closely related to the palaces at Pasargadae and Persepolis and is completely different from the usual Babylonian open-court construction (Fig. 8). It consists of an oblong, hypostyle audience room with a pillared portico, which is flanked by square towers. While the bases of the four columns in the portico consist of a simple torus, those from the hypostyle chamber (2x4) are bell-shaped and are decorated with egg shapes and stylised leaves (Fig. 9). These decorated bases are typically Achaemenian: they are made of a greyish-black stone which might possibly have originated in an Iranian quarry. Nothing remains of the column shafts, which were probably made of wood.

The exterior walls, and perhaps also others, of this palace were decorated with panels of glazed bricks illustrating the 'Ten Thousand Immortals', the king's picked troops, the finest in the empire (Pl. 5).[2] They are shown clad in long, rich tunics. They wear fine bracelets and are equipped with bows, quivers and long spears. Some are represented life-size, while others are only half life-size, and some panels are executed in relief while others are flat. Other decorated tiles and bricks found in the palace originally belonged to the ceiling and the stairways. They are decorated with cuneiform inscriptions and with a rich variety of motifs, mainly floral and geometric patterns (Fig. 10). Not only is the iconography on the glazed panels completely different from that of the Neo-Babylonian period which decorated the Ishtar Gate, but so are the technical features. The bricks and tiles are not made of clay, as were their Neo-Babylonian counterparts, but are composed of a mixture of sand and lime. Furthermore, the range of colours on the Achaemenid tiles and bricks is much richer and more varied: we find white, blue, yellow, green, brown and black, but not red. The tiles and bricks which decorated this small Babylonian palace are identical in all respects to those found at Susa and Persepolis. Fragments of the same greyish-black stone as that used for the column bases are unfortunately too badly preserved to permit reconstruction. They do indicate, however, that there were sculptured stone panels decorated with human, as well as floral motifs. The original floor of the palace has survived. It is 60 cm thick and consists of a kind of red concrete-like deposit. Such floors also occur at Susa and Persepolis (Stoops and Stoops 1994).

A fine white limestone impost block, shaped like the foreparts of two bulls but unfortunately badly mutilated, was found in the East Court of the Southern Citadel on the Kasr mound. It might also belong to the Achaemenid period. There is no doubt that Achaemenid influence can most easily be found in palaces, demonstrating once again that Achaemenid art is mainly an expression of royal power and is reflected in the construction of these imposing buildings.

We must also mention the discovery of campaniform bases at Abu Chulfat, Hatab (Pl. 6). This is approximately some 40 km to the south-east of Nippur and 11 km north of Fara, but the exact location of this site is no longer known (Wetzel *et al.* 1957: 25, pl. 26 a–b). It is deplorable that there is no further information available about this site. Another column base has been found at Musedjir, in Kurdistan (Fig. 11; Boehmer 1973: 491); and from Tell ed-Deim, to the north-east of Kirkuk comes an undecorated torus (al-Tekriti 1960: pl. 11).

In addition to impressive religious and palatial buildings, excavations have revealed more humble dwellings as well as a variety of objects. However, because the Persians did not sack any cities and there are, therefore, no destruction levels, it is not always easy to date the objects precisely. Herodotus describes the Babylonians as being perfumed and wearing long linen tunics under a woollen tunic and a short white cloak. Their hair was long and was covered with a kind of tall hat or cap. This is almost exactly how they are depicted on the famous Apadana reliefs at Persepolis. From excavations we also know that they wore safety-pins or brooches (fibulae), and earrings and bracelets made of iron, bronze and silver. Women wore anklets as well. Gold is rare (Pl. 7; Otto 1944). Herodotus also mentions (I.195) that each Babylonian had his own seal. These were probably stamp seals or rings with engraved bezels rather than cylinder seals, for during the Achaemenid period the latter were relatively little used. In addition to the traditional Mesopotamian motifs used to decorate seals, such as a man standing in front of an altar, new motifs were introduced by the Persians (Fig. 12; Legrain 1925: 45–8; Zettler 1979). These included the winged sun-disc, perhaps representing the principal god of the Persian pantheon, Ahura Mazda, people in Persian dress, and the hero-king killing beasts. From Egypt comes the representation of the god Bes.

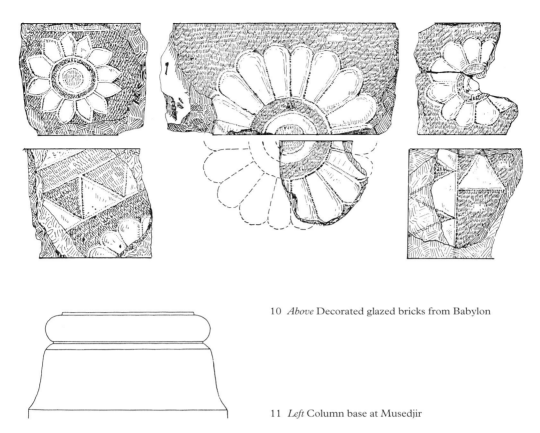

10 *Above* Decorated glazed bricks from Babylon

11 *Left* Column base at Musedjir

Everyday items such as pottery vessels were very common, and large storage jars have been found in houses. There was also a wide variety of plates, bowls, cups, jars and pitchers. Characteristic of the Achaemenid period in southern Mesopotamia and south-western Iran were deep, thin-walled bowls (Fleming 1989). Both glazed pottery and glass vessels (Barag 1968) were relatively rare and should be considered as luxury objects, while alabaster bowls and flasks, sometimes with cuneiform inscriptions, probably belonged to high-ranking officials (von Bissing 1942; Schmitt 1975; Gropp 1979). Metal vessels are not well represented in excavations. In a hoard found at Babylon, however, was a tubular amphora handle made of silver and showing a winged bull (Pl. 8; Robinson 1950 : 47–8, pl. XXIII; Reade 1986 : 80, pl. II). It is from a vessel of the same type as those shown on the Persepolis reliefs. From the same hoard, perhaps from a silversmith's shop, came fragments of bowls with floral patterns. The scarcity of precious metal in Achaemenid Mesopotamia may be explained as a consequence of the high taxes imposed by the Achaemenids, which created a metal shortage. While coins were current in western parts of the Achaemenid empire, they are nearly totally lacking in Mesopotamia and Iran, where the old traditions of weighing fragments of gold and silver, or simply exchanging goods, were still current (Joannès 1994). Some coins were present in the hoard found at Babylon (Robinson 1950: 44–7).

12 Seal impressions on Achaemenid period cuneiform tablets from Babylonia

Figurines made of terracotta are numerous on all sites in the Ancient Near East. Although their dating is not well established, some types were particularly common at certain periods. Two types were popular in Babylonia during the Achaemenid period. First there is a horse and rider which measures *c*. 8–15 cm in height and which is sometimes painted (Pl. 9; Koldewey 1914: fig. 150; Reuther 1926: fig. 42). The man usually has an oval-shaped face, a moustache, a long beard, a pronounced nose and wears a pointed cap. The function of these figurines can only be guessed at: some authorities consider them to be religious objects, while others think they were toys. They have been found in temples as well as in houses and graves. Although they were first produced early in the first half of the first millennium BC, they were particularly common in the Achaemenid period, not only in Mesopotamia but throughout the

Near East. There were also female figurines, including some showing a woman suckling a baby. Particularly typical of the Achaemenid period are statuettes showing women riding on horseback (Pl.10; Koldewey 1914: fig. 151; Reuther 1926: fig. 43).

The dead were buried within the city walls, usually in a ruined building (Strommenger 1964). Various types of burial occur in the Achaemenid period: these include simple earth burials where the body is covered by a reed mat or potsherds, and pot-graves. The most typical practice, however, is interment in sarcophagi, which are either like a bath tub or a distinctive keyhole-shaped trough. The latter were used either upright or upside-down. For use in the afterlife, the body was accompanied by a selection of small objects, including bracelets, figurines, seals and pottery plates and flasks. It should be remembered, however, that no rich burials have as yet been found in Babylon. Two important burials deserve particular mention. These are the rock-cut tombs of Qizqapan and Kur-u-Kich situated in north-eastern Iraq, close to Surdash, on the road from Sulaimaniya to the Dokan Dam (Edmonds 1934: 183–9, figs 14, pls XXIII–XXVI). There are cogent reasons for believing that both belong to the Achaemenid era, as suggested by, for example, H. von Gall (1988). The Qizqapan tomb is cut into a rock face about 7.5 m above ground level; it is 7.13 m wide, *c.* 5 m high and 2.78 m deep. The façade (7.58 m wide) is sculpted like the entrance to a building with two Ionic half-columns; there is a door in between and a roof-like cover carved in the rock and imitating beams (Fig. 13). The door gives access to three burial chambers, in which the coffins are hollowed out of the rock. These coffins do not seem to be big enough to contain the outstretched body of a grown person, so they should rather be seen as astodans, in which the bones of the dead were gathered. The decoration above the door is especially interesting. Two men are

13 Rock-cut grave at Qizqapan.

33

depicted with a stepped fire-altar between them. Each man raises his right hand. In his left hand each holds a bow which rests on the tip of the foot. Both men wear the Median dress and the man on the left is also clad in the typical Median *kandys* (a characteristic dress with long sleeves, closed at the ends). Both have a *bashlyk* on their head. Above the fire-altar and between the two Ionic capitals there is carved decoration consisting of a circle with the crescent of the moon and a bearded figure, who probably represents the Persian moon-god Mah. On the left side of the façade there is the figure of a four-winged symbol, which could represent Ahura Mazda or a protective god. On the right side there is the representation of a star with eleven rays, which is difficult to interpret. H. von Gall recently dated this grave to the period between the late fifth century BC and the end of the Achaemenid dynasty; other scholars would prefer to place it in the Hellenistic period. The smaller grave (width 6.75 m, height 4.05 m, depth 2.40 m) of Kur-u-Kich is located 2–3 km to the south of Qizqapan (Edmonds 1934: 190–92, figs 5–7, pl. xxvii). It is again cut out of the rock but is undecorated, with two semi-engaged columns on either side of the door and a rather small funerary chamber.

On the whole, we must admit that our knowledge of the material culture of Mesopotamia during the Achaemenid period is far from complete. It is to be hoped that new excavations using modern techniques will give us a better picture of everyday life. The information now available mainly demonstrates Persian presence in Babylonia in royal palaces as well as showing Persian influence on luxury goods. Babylon and other cities continued to thrive under foreign rule and enjoyed a rich and flourishing cultural life. In due course Alexander the Great decided to make Babylon one of the centres of his empire. Old traditions gradually changed and the area adapted to a new way of life under Greek rule.

Notes
1 See also Haerinck 1987, 1990a, 1990b.
2 See also Metzler 1975.

Anshan and Parsa: Early Achaemenid History, Art and Architecture on the Iranian Plateau

by David Stronach

UNIVERSITY OF CALIFORNIA, BERKELEY

As recently as a few decades ago most authorities tended to view Achaemenid art as a static phenomenon. It was perceived as an entity that had been invented within a few brief years and which subsequently continued to reproduce itself, virtually unchanged, through a span of more than two centuries. The first modification of this monolithic interpretation came when it was recognised that the art of the time of Cyrus the Great (559–530 BC) was indeed different in many critical respects from that of Darius the Great (522–486 BC) and that it could be useful, in terms of broad definitions, to separate 'archaic' Achaemenid art from 'classic' Achaemenid art (cf. Stronach 1978: 106). More recently, it has also been pointed out that the diverse forms of Achaemenid Persian art that found expression within the vast multicultural realm of the Achaemenids during the period between, say, the death of Darius I and the sack of Persepolis in 330 BC, were themselves subject to varying degrees of change (Root 1995: 2615).

In the present enquiry we will in fact be most concerned to re-examine – albeit in a preliminary fashion – the causes of the division that can be so clearly discerned between the art of Cyrus and that of Darius. It is an enquiry that will attempt, not least, to explore the circumstances that, on the one hand, led Cyrus and his forebears to invoke Teispes and the Land of Anshan as the chief touchstones of a proud royal heritage and, on the other hand, made Achaemenes (a putative predecessor of Teispes) and possession of the Land of Parsa, not Anshan, the equivalent verities of the line of Darius.

Beginnings in Fars

Not the least puzzling aspect of the early history of Fars – the region of south-west Iran to

35

which the ancient Persians first gave their name – is the rarity on the ground of any physical evidence that would appear to substantiate a Persian presence in the area before the middle of the sixth century BC. To judge, for example, from other patterns of Indo-European penetration in adjacent parts of the Near East (such as that which is illustrated by the use of Indo-Aryan words at a time consonant with the rise of the sixteenth century BC and later Mitannian kingdom), Indo-European Iranian speakers could have begun to arrive in western Iran anywhere within the course of the second millennium BC (Muscarella 1995: 984).

Where the Persians themselves are concerned, however, the Assyrians first met groups of Persians in the valleys of the central Zagros in 844 BC (Grayson 1996). Partly for this reason it is generally assumed that the main body of the Persians would have reached the more southerly region of Fars by a somewhat similar date. Just such a reconstruction might be supported, moreover, by the evident decline of the city of Anshan (Fig. 14), the one-time highland capital of Elam, at a date near 1000 BC and, still more emphatically, by the final abandonment of Anshan (and Darvazeh Tepe, the only contemporary excavated site in the same region) at a time that can hardly be placed any later than 850 BC (Carter 1994: 66).

Critical to any examination of these hypothetical conjunctions is, of course, the early first

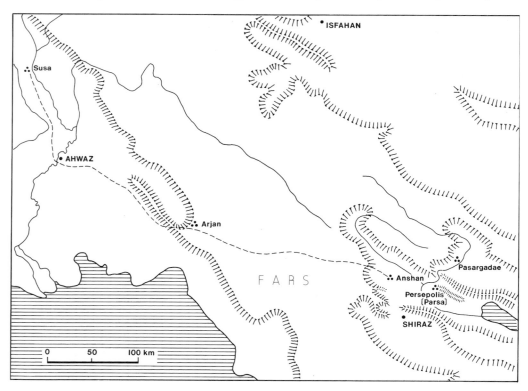

14 Map of south-western Iran. The interlocking valleys in the vicinity of Shiraz constitute the core area of the fertile highland region that has been known, at successive intervals, as Anshan, Parsa and Fars. Like Anshan of old, Parsa (Persepolis) shared the name of the territory within which it stood.

millennium BC archaeological record as a whole for the Marv Dasht or 'The Grassy Plain', the majestic valley at the heart of Fars which was also home to the venerable city of Anshan. In this context W. Sumner's exacting field surveys in the Marv Dasht have shown that the frequently co-occurring plain and painted wares of the local, mainly second millennium, Shoga and Teimuran ceramic traditions failed to endure much beyond 900 BC (Sumner 1994: 101). But while this pattern accords with the above-mentioned hints of significant change near the beginning of the first millennium BC, it remains quite remarkable that there is then a gap of several hundred years in the record of permanent settlement throughout the Marv Dasht. Indeed, when settlement resumes (often in line with the distribution of earlier sites in the valley), it only appears to do so – of a certitude – during the fifth and fourth centuries BC, i.e. well within the period of imperial Achaemenid rule.

If some attempt should be made to reconstruct at least part of the broad picture that would then be suggested by a combination of the above archaeological evidence and certain well attested historical events, it would seem possible that, in the first instance, the arrival of the Persians (in the shape of pastoralists making their way down from the north) served to introduce – perhaps only after centuries of gradual infiltration – a number of substantial changes in local settlement patterns c. 900 BC. In a second stage (coeval with the Neo-Elamite revival which began c. 750 BC and which lasted for just over a hundred years), there are grounds for concluding that the rulers of lowland Elam actively aspired to renewed control in Fars. Evidence to this effect comes not only from the seventh century BC Elamite relief that came to be carved at one point on the cliff face at Naqsh-i Rustam, but also from the fact that the kings of Elam continued to use the long-sanctified title, 'King of Anshan and Susa', down to the middle years of the seventh century (Miroschedji 1985: 278–80). At the same time, however, the effectiveness of Neo-Elamite control in the east may well have been episodic at best, especially during the forty-five year period between the close of the 690s (when the Neo-Elamite kingdom's conflicts with Assyria began in earnest) and the year 646 BC when the army of Ashurbanipal succeeded in capturing and destroying the city of Susa.[1]

The line of Teispes as an Anshanite Dynasty

It is against this background that the genealogical testimony of the so-called Cyrus cylinder (Pl. 11) sheds further vital light on the history of Fars in the second quarter of the first millennium BC. In this document, which was drawn up in Akkadian (presumably for local consumption) soon after the fall of Babylon in 539 BC, Cyrus asserts that he was the 'son of Cambyses, Great King, King of Anshan, grandson of Cyrus, Great King, King of Anshan, descendant of Teispes, Great King, King of Anshan, of a family [which] always [exercised] kingship' (Pritchard 1955: 316). For all too long, however, the world of scholarship has found it difficult to come to terms with the unlooked for presence of the word 'Anshan' in this titulary. Even though the Babylonian Chronicle had already used the terms Anshan and Parsa in a virtually interchangeable fashion some ten years earlier,[2] it has been speculated that Cyrus might have instructed the scribes of Babylon to use the ancient toponym 'Anshan' in order to make the distant, highland homeland of the Persians more immediately familiar to the Mesopotamian audience for which the text was intended. Then again, in yet another interpretation, the use of 'Anshan' in the Cyrus cylinder (as opposed to that of 'Parsa' in the inscriptions of Darius) was taken to be a reflection of a prior state of affairs in which the older line of Cyrus the Great had installed itself in Anshan while the 'younger' line of Darius had ruled over a separate, more easterly region, Parsa. This once widely touted 'equal division of the Persian kingdom' was shown to be untenable, however, when Tall-i Malyan, only 50 km north-west of Persepolis (Fig. 14), was found to be the lost city of Anshan (Hansman 1972; Reiner 1973). At that juncture, in the early 1970s, it was at last evident that Anshan and Parsa were effectively no more than different names for one and the same stretch of territory and that the longstanding pre-eminence of the forefathers of Cyrus could no longer be disputed (Stronach 1974b:248).

It has also become evident in recent years that the use of the term Anshan in the just-quoted titulary of Cyrus was not in any sense an aberration. A number of the fortification tablets from Persepolis carry the imprint of a cylinder seal of distinctly older date (Fig. 15); and, on the basis of this seal's inscription, which can be translated from the Elamite as 'Cyrus, the Anshanite, son of Teispes' (Hallock 1969; 1977; Zettler, 1979: 266), it is now possible to assert that the predecessors of Cyrus consistently identified themselves with the age-old Elamite name for highland south-west Iran, namely 'Anshan', and that, just as consistently, they regarded the true founder of their dynastic line as Teispes or, as the name is more accurately rendered in Old Persian, Chishpish.[3]

More interesting still is the fact that the genealogies that appear in the above-mentioned cylinder seal and in the Cyrus cylinder make no mention of Achaemenes, the remote figure with an unmistakably Persian name who is named by Darius as the eponymous founder of the Achaemenid royal family. Apart from the fact that Achaemenes finds no mention before the reign of Darius, the names Teispes (Chishpish) and Cyrus (OP Kurush) are each without a discernible Persian etymology. And while little has so far been done to examine the name of Teispes, the difficulty of finding anything other than an Elamite origin for the name Cyrus has been a subject of debate for close to a century (cf. Frye 1962: 266, n. 50). In recent years, moreover, R. Zadok has indicated that Elamite *Kurash* adjusted to Old Persian *kuru-* provides the nominative *Kurush* (Zadok 1991: 237) and that the Neo-Elamite verb *kur* carries the meaning 'to bestow care' (Zadok 1995: 246). Accordingly, the original Elamite name, Kurash, could well have had the attractive meaning of 'he who bestows care'.

The line of Teispes as an increasingly Persian dynasty

Apart from a definite need to acknowledge the Anshanite sense of dynastic identity that was probably common to all members of the line of Teispes down to the demise of its last two representatives, Cambyses II (530–522 BC) and Bardiya, the two short-lived sons of Cyrus the Great, it is only appropriate to recognise the extent to which this seemingly autochthonous dynasty took on an increasingly Persian character from at least the middle of the seventh century BC onwards. The first indication of this significant development in the history of the dynasty could well come from the annals of the Assyrian monarch, Ashurbanipal (668–627 BC). It is through these records that we learn that, in the aftermath of the fall of Susa, a certain Cyrus (with the spelling Kurash) 'of Parsumash' was obliged to send his son, Arukku, as a hostage to Nineveh. As G. Cameron has surmised (1936: 213), Arukku's presence at Nineveh was probably designed to deter any thoughts of dangerous aggrandisement that might have occurred to Arukku's father as he contemplated the defeated and defenceless remnant of Elam.

At the same time, however, the central fascination of this particular entry in the annals is the fact that the Assyrians viewed Arukku and his father as coming (as the name Parsumash indicates) from a *Persian* entity. And while there can be no absolute certainty that 'Cyrus of Parsumash' was a direct ancestor of Cyrus the Great, there has to be, at least in my estimation, a strong presumption that this was the case.[4] Furthermore, it is increasingly tempting to associate this seemingly assertive 'Persian' ruler with the spirited 'Anshanite' Cyrus (or Kurash) of the royal seal impression shown in Fig. 15.

If we had more complete records for the earliest stages of the dynasty of Teispes we might also discover that the owner of the seal, himself the son of the founder of the line, was not a mere grandfather of Cyrus the Great but a great-grandfather or (if we insert yet another Cambyses) a great-great-grandfather of the founder of Pasargadae. But it is probably fruitless to speculate further on this one score. What is at least clear is that the name change from Kurash to Kurush could have been introduced because of the increasingly Persian character of the dynasty[5] and that, while Cyrus the Great appears to have followed dynastic tradition in giving his eldest son the same name of uncertain derivation as that held by his father (i.e. Cambyses or OP Kambujiya), the known names of his other immediate family members (including that of Bardiya) are each unequivocally Persian.

The accession of Darius I

According to the testimony of his long and detailed Bisitun inscription, it fell to Darius, a member of a cadet branch of the royal family, to restore the throne to its rightful heirs when Cambyses II, the son of Cyrus the Great, died without issue. Nonetheless there is much in Darius' account of his origins that fails to carry a ring of conviction:

> 'My father was Hystaspes; Hystaspes' father was Arsames; Arsames' father was
> Ariaramnes; Ariaramnes' father was Teispes; Teispes' father was Achaemenes. Said
> Darius the King: For this reason we are called the Achaemenids.'

As has been recently observed (Sancisi-Weerdenburg 1995: 1038), it sounds 'as if the family name was used to create a founding father in order to achieve contemporary legitimacy'. More than this, of course, the stratagem of placing Achaemenes before Teispes had the effect of making each member of the line of Cyrus a member of the now all-embracing Achaemenid family. Thus, at one stroke, a new, seamless Achaemenid Persian past was called into being.

It was a vision that has proved uncommonly durable. And, whatever the actual complexities may have been, it may still make broad historical sense, not least in art historical terms, to adhere to the notion of an Achaemenid Persian continuum from the early seventh century BC down to the death of Darius III in 330 BC (for which scheme, see also note 6 below).

To return, however, to our exploration of those factors which may help to account for the visible divide between the imagery of Cyrus and Darius, Cyrus seems to have been imbued with certain traditional norms of Near Eastern thought that were probably not only proper to the region of Fars but also to many other parts of western Iran through much of the seventh and sixth centuries BC. I also like to think that Cyrus may have been conscious of a certain element of continuity in the way that his royal stewardship evolved, from ruling a heterogeneous population (with at least two languages and two sets of religious beliefs) in his own homeland of Fars to ruling a far more disparate collection of peoples with many more languages, customs and beliefs. There is also much to indicate that he remained uniquely ready to delegate substantial degrees of military and/or administrative authority to experienced individuals from amongst those whom he conquered.

In an era of rapid change and, most especially, in a period which must have seen an increasingly significant change in the attitudes of a core body of high-ranking Persian officials close to the person of the king, Cyrus' mid-sixth century tenets were obviously not destined to last forever. And Darius, in looking for new-sprung props to his rule following his assumption of power, appears to have had a remarkable ability to target many of the most closely felt desires and ambitions of his Persian subjects. It is in accord with these dynamics, in short, that a new, expressly Persian definition of homeland, kingship, and religion begins to find unambiguous textual and visual articulation from 522 BC onwards.

With particular reference, then, to the earliest available forms of Persian art, we will conclude this survey by citing a number of examples of what may be referred to, at least in provisional terms, as Proto-Achaemenid, Early Achaemenid, and Mature Achaemenid art.[6]

Proto-Achaemenid art (c. 675–550 BC)

No small degree of interest necessarily attaches to the one (previously mentioned) item that can definitely be ascribed to the earlier half of this quite long interval. The collated seal impression in question (Fig. 15) shows an equestrian figure in the act of spearing an opponent while two slain foes already lie, arms akimbo, on the ground. While various elements link this cylinder seal design to contemporary Neo-Elamite seal designs, it can in fact be seen to be representative of a distinctive Proto-Achaemenid glyptic style, which includes a deft control of modelling and a 'light and airy' sense of composition (Garrison 1991: 6; cf. also Bollweg 1988: 53f.). From an early fifth century BC perspective it is intriguing to wonder, moreover, if not just the content of the inscription but also the nature of the design, with what could have been viewed as a striking anticipation of two of Darius's more memorable textual images – that of the far-travelled 'spear of a Persian man' and that of a monarch who was skilled as a spearman 'afoot and on horseback' (Kent 1953: 138–40) – could have encouraged the use of this specific heirloom at Persepolis.

15 *Left* Line drawing of the collated image of a cylinder seal which carried an inscription, 'Kurash, the Anshanite, son of Teispes'. Mid-seventh century BC.

16 *Right* Bronze stand from a tomb at Arjan, near modern Behbehan. Early sixth century BC.

If the art of the first half of this formative period can already be said to reveal an intriguing sense of innovation and experiment, the art of the second half of the period appears to take us considerably further down the road towards the canons of later, more instantly recognisable Achaemenid taste. In the latter context, the only excavated evidence comes from a Neo-Elamite royal tomb at Arjan which, if we are dealing with a single, undisturbed burial, may date to 600 BC or a little later (Curtis 1995: 22).

To judge from the contents of the Arjan tomb (which was situated in highland, eastern Elam at a point roughly halfway between Susa and Anshan), this was a time of complex cultural interaction when Babylonian, Assyrian, Syrian, Elamite, and Iranian stylistic traditions were each present in south-western Iran (cf. Carter 1994: 76). It is tempting to suppose, in fact, that it was just such a kaleidoscope of styles and motifs that provided the necessary stimulus for those experiments that led, in due course, to the measured rhythms of evolved Achaemenid taste. In one work that clearly reflects diverse influences, for example, the kneeling bull protomes at the base of a tall bronze stand (Fig. 16) are already strongly suggestive of the norms of later Achaemenid animal art.

Early Achaemenid Art (550–522 BC)

As far as this more familiar period of Achaemenid history is concerned, most of the extant evidence comes, of course, from Pasargadae, the capital of Cyrus the Great. And even if it cannot be our purpose in this forum to rehearse the full range of diverse influences on the art and architecture of this exceptional site, it will be pertinent to draw attention to just a few select features, where one or another observation may add force to some of the new Elamite, or, more particularly, local west Iranian, perspectives that have hitherto received only limited notice.

With reference to that most durable and successful of monuments, the tomb of Cyrus (Pl. 12), it has often been argued that the tomb's high, stepped plinth ought to owe the lower part of its distinctive design to the stepped profile of a Mesopotamian ziggurat. In reality, however, Cyrus is more likely (if any part of the design can claim such an inspiration) to have been

17 Gate R, Pasargadae. The winged figure.

citing a tradition of ziggurat construction that was closer to home: namely that which was known from Elam (Ghirshman 1966). If we think of the massive tiers of the tomb, and the prominent grove of trees that originally surrounded the monument, it is possible to suppose that Cyrus could have been intent on quoting both the tiers of a stepped temple platform *and* the trees of a hallowed 'sacred grove' (for which unusual Elamite phenomenon, see now Vallat 1995: 1031). In this latter context it is perhaps instructive to recall Strabo's account of Alexander's visit to Pasargadae (*Geography* xv.3.7). There we are told that Alexander saw the tomb of Cyrus 'in a paradise, a tower of no great size, *concealed* [my emphasis] beneath the thicket of trees, in its lower parts massive, but its upper parts having a roof and a shrine, with a very narrow entrance'.

However this may be, one of the chief advertisements of the scale of dominion that Cyrus came to command was the absence of any major wall surrounding his capital. This circumstance gave him no option but to devise a new, freestanding form of monumental entrance. This consisted of a tall hypostyle hall furnished with two main and two side doorways. In a design that was later partly repeated by Darius at Persepolis, the outer doorway of Gate R was flanked by a pair of winged bulls while a pair of winged human-headed bulls faced toward the palaces.

Since the core of this monument consisted of a standard eight-columned Iranian hall (a type of structure that was probably common to local courts throughout much of highland western Iran in the seventh and sixth centuries BC), one of Cyrus' initiatives was to give this long-hallowed form (Col. Pl. v) the unexpected character of an entryway.[7]

A second arresting element in this new design was the nature of the winged human genius (Fig. 17) that came to be carved on the stone jambs of at least one of Gate R's opposed side doorways (cf. Stronach 1978: 55). While it appears to have been ultimately based on a late eighth-century type of winged genius that is known from Khorsabad (Pl. 13), the Winged Figure of Gate R is nonetheless firmly anchored in its mid sixth-century time-frame by its now full-profile pose, its smooth musculature, and its distinct, Persian physiognomy.

Apart from its calm, grave face, the most notable (and somewhat oddly juxtaposed) attributes of the Gate R genius include its four straight-tipped Assyrian wings, its divine crown of Egyptian origin, and its long, fringed Elamite robe. Of these various attributes, it is necessarily the last that must most concern us at this time.

As is well known, the fringed robe of the Winged Figure finds its best parallel in the costume of the mid seventh-century Elamite ruler, Tepti-Khumban-Inshushinak (Te-Umman in the Akkadian texts), whose defeat and ignominious death represent the central theme in the reliefs at Nineveh that record the battle of Til-Tuba on the banks of the Ulai river. For this reason, certain authorities have speculated that this same form of dress could have been worn down to the time of Cyrus himself (Barnett 1969: 420). This is most unlikely, however. In the Bisitun relief no such archaic royal costume is in evidence – and each of the depicted opponents of Darius with a manifest connection with Persia and/or Elam can be seen to have been dressed in the same voluminous, partly pleated costume as that worn by Darius and his two Persian supporters. In short, this appears to have been a standard form of élite dress in both Persia and Elam for quite some time before the reign of Cyrus.

In these circumstances it is now possible to suggest that this particular costume (even if Cyrus, son of Teispes, had little use for it as a riding habit) was intended to draw attention to certain still well-remembered Anshanite elements in the past history of Cyrus's line. In other words – in contrast to the closely copied Assyrian colossi of the two main doorways – the Winged Figure provided (or was intended to provide) a *partly local* element in the programme of supernatural protection that was drawn up to protect Gate R and, by extension, the site of Pasargadae as a whole.

The almost complete preservation of the Winged Figure also allows us to make certain other observations. In particular, the distinctive treatment of the facial features provides a timely reminder that the sculpture of the Early Achaemenid period was, in essence, far, far closer to the art of Darius than to the art of Assyria. This is what we should expect, but it is not always stressed. The calm demeanour of this eclectic, apotropaic figure also helps to illustrate the fact that the pacific tenor of Achaemenid palace art begins with Cyrus's pioneer sculptural programme at Pasargadae; and, in terms of palace art, it is worth recalling that this estimable quality was never abandoned.

The last sculptures of special relevance in this survey of Early Achaemenid art are those which flank the opposed north-west and south-east doorways of Palace S. In so far as they can be judged from their present, fragmentary condition (in which they are seldom preserved much above the level of the knee), they constitute relatively closely copied examples of some of the most arresting apotropaic figures known from the Late Assyrian repertoire. The caveat 'relatively closely copied' stems from the fact that (a) the musculature of these figures appears to have been softened to suit the less obviously muscled character of all Persian sculpture and (b) the fact that certain of the figures were almost definitely portrayed without their character-istic Assyrian equipment (such as a bucket and cone).

The paired figures on the opposed jambs of the north-west doorway consist, in Assyrian terms, of the smiting god followed by the lion-demon (Fig. 18). This pairing is not only common in Assyrian art in general (Black and Green 1992: 165; Green 1994: 251), but it is also expressly found in certain of the doorway reliefs in the palace of Sennacherib at Nineveh (Fig. 19). In the south-east doorway of Palace S, on the other hand, the association of the fish-garbed man and the bull-man (Pl. 14) is not representative of any known Assyrian pair-ing, even if the fish-garbed man is found in the company of other protective, colossal beings in the monumental reliefs of the palace of Sennacherib in at least three instances (Kawami 1972: 147) and even if the apotropaic qualities of the bull-man are otherwise widely attested (Wiggerman 1992: 179). It may be added that large-scale fish-garbed figures were also placed, in splendid isolation, on the opposed door jambs of at least one doorway in Sen-nacherib's palace (Kawami 1972, pls IIIa–b) – and that wherever the type appears to have been charged with an apotropaic function it necessarily has to be thought of as a supernatural

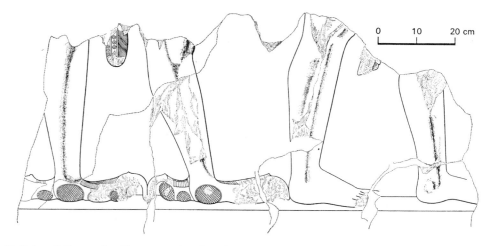

18 Palace S, Pasargadae. Extant remains of a relief showing the paired figures of the 'smiting god' followed by the 'lion-demon'.

protective being (as opposed to a mere human agent, garbed for ritual purposes).

When it comes to interpreting the significance of these sculptures from Palace S, it is particularly important, I believe, not to rush to judgement. That is to say, that while the giant bull colossi of Gate R were perhaps mainly intended to underscore the fact that Cyrus had fallen heir to the dominion of Assyria in its halcyon days, the message of the Palace S reliefs may well have been more subtle and more complex. Even if the available evidence from late Iron Age Iran is less complete than we might wish it to be, it already seems highly likely that Assyrian, or Assyrian-related, magical protective images were well known and well appreciated in western Iran from at least the seventh century BC onwards.[8] Accordingly, Cyrus may have found it especially appropriate to draw on the rich vein of protective Assyrian imagery *not* for what it would have meant to any contemporary visitor from Mesopotamia or points still further to the west, but rather for the messages of power and legitimacy that it would have spelt out to members of his extended 'home constituency' in western Iran. Cyrus' subjects from this latter region were probably not only familiar with various extant renderings of such images in local court settings, but they may even have been acquainted with still intact Assyrian wall paintings such as those at Til Barsip in north Syria (Parrot 1961: figs 109–10) in one-time outposts of Assyrian provincial government within the central Zagros.

Cyrus was also in a position, moreover, to insist on certain requirements which underscore what would seem to have been his abiding search for perfection in all aspects of monumental construction. That is to say, he could order the most skilled members of his building force to return to the original sources of such Assyrian imagery, i.e. to the partly ruined palaces of Sargon and Sennacherib, in order to make close copies of the original models (cf. Curtis and Reade 1995: fig. 41); and, in this way, his highly trained sculptors were presumably able to adapt each of the selected images to the latest norms of Early Achaemenid taste.

19 Divine guardians from the palace of
Sennacherib at Nineveh.

Mature Achaemenid art (522–330 BC)

It is within this interval, and especially within the thirty-six year reign of Darius I, that numerous innovations document the emergence of a new artistic sensibility that is unequivocally distinct from any that existed beforehand. From one perspective such innovations serve to illustrate how much can be owed to no more than a single, exceptionally gifted 'royal architect' and from another the tumultuous political climate of the last quarter of the sixth century BC can be said to bear witness to the extent to which a particular set of historical circumstances (such as those that we have just reviewed) can sometimes spur the construction of a prodigal range of monuments.

In the present context we will do no more than note the first, most obvious steps that Darius took (expressly with reference to his monuments on the Iranian Plateau) to give clear, especially visual articulation to (a) Ahuramazda's endorsement of this rule, (b) his elevation to royal status, and (c) his Achaemenid Persian identity.

Divine endorsement of the rule of Darius

Since the Bisitun relief (Col. Pl. IV), carved c. 520 BC, was intended to provide a kind of visual synopsis of the events that brought Darius to power, and since the accompanying text repeatedly asserts that the 'favour' of the god Ahuramazda made the kingship of Darius possible, Darius instantly had far more reason than any previous ruler in Iran to introduce an image of this same deity. In such circumstances it was only logical for him to turn, as others had before him, to the rich repertoire of Assyrian iconography (which by this time was probably more at home in Iran than anywhere else in the Near East) for a suitably enduring image.

Nevertheless, the haste that was inherent in the sudden determination to give visual, sculpted form to a deity that had most probably not been defined in visual terms on any prior occasion is clearly apparent. Thus it is evident that the circular device at the top of the crown was not part of Darius' original composition. Instead, this element was introduced – as a conscious addition to the original design – on the surface of an inset stone cube that can be seen to have been secured (as was one other inset in another part of the relief) by a metal spike (Pl.16).

As to the divine form that was borrowed from the Assyrian sculptural corpus, Darius shrewdly selected the regal half-figure of Shamash, the sun god (and god of justice), whose form emerges from a winged disc and who was often represented in this guise as hovering above the king or above the monarch's doubled image. All the same, the circular device that protrudes from the top of Ahuramazda's crown is definitely not a copy of Shamash's distinctive solar disc (Black and Green 1992: fig. 73) and, since so many other elements in the Bisitun relief appear to have been inspired by the neighbouring twenty-first- or twentieth-century BC rock relief of King Anubanini near Sar-i Pul (Fig. 20), Darius may have based this rayed symbol on the over-sized star of Inanna that appears between Anubanini and the awkwardly 'hovering' figure of Inanna herself. It also deserves to be stressed that, just as Anubanini's relief can be interpreted as both a victory relief and an investiture relief, so is this the case with

20 Rock relief of King Anubanini (*c.*2000 BC), located 150 km west of Bisitun at Sar-i Pul.

regard to Darius' great relief. Today this detail is possibly less obvious than it would have been in the past, since Darius, in yet another imaginative departure, would seem to have ordered a gold 'ring of kingship' to be affixed to the rock in the apparent grasp of Ahuramazda's left hand.[9]

Visual documentation of Darius' royal status

Whether or not Cyrus had it in mind to introduce his own likeness on the door jambs of the main doorways of Palace P at Pasargadae during the last phases of the construction of that building (which was still at a very early stage of construction at the time of his death), Darius presumably knew that he could ill afford to wait for anything approaching a similar length of time within his own reign before defining (and broadcasting) an imposing image of himself as king. He would have been well aware of the urgent need to advertise, in visual terms, his newly acquired royal station, his defeat of his principal opponents (a disproportionate number of whom came from a Persian or Elamite background), and the degree of direct Persian support that had helped him to secure his claim to the throne (cf. especially DB IV 68; Kent 1953: 132). In each of these areas the Bisitun monument provides a detailed record of Darius' extraordinary reach for power following the unexpected death of Cambyses II in 522 BC.

At least one of the areas of experimentation that can be detected in the Bisitun relief has already been identified. The record is just as instructive where the representation of the dress of Darius, that of his two weapon bearers and, most notably, that of the recumbent Gaumata is concerned. The robes of these various figures provide the earliest, most detailed depictions of the multi-folded, voluminous Persian dress; collectively, in fact, they document the contrasted 'naturalistic' and 'stylised' representations of dress (Pl. 17) that were then being tested by the royal sculptors (cf. Stronach 1978: 96 ff.). The conventions of Mature Achaemenid art were also far from set in other ways. That is to say that, while Darius' unnamed (but conceivably noble) attendants were in one sense portrayed as no more than royal weapon bearers, they were otherwise allowed to appear uncharacteristically close in character and in finery to the figure of the king.

One other iconographical innovation was quite possibly contemplated, at least for a brief interval. As Pl. 18 indicates, distinct cut marks are visible along the top and down at least one side of the lower part of the beard of Darius. To begin with I thought it conceivable that Darius might have been depicted with the same kind of short beard as that which is found on the face of each of his followers, and that a secondary stone inset had then been introduced in order to give him a full-length beard. On further reflection, however, I cannot believe that this was the case. Not only does the original stone still look to have been very probably left in place, but Darius's dominant pose and stature (not to mention the tone of his inscription) could never have called for anything other than a beard of regal proportions.

So what 'afterthoughts' could have inspired this apparently aborted attempt to remove the original beard? The simplest explanation, of course, would have been the belated discovery of a possible flaw in the stone and, hence, a perceived need to replace the block in question. But since no defect in the stone is readily apparent, it may be more appropriate to ask if this exercise had something to do with the pace at which sculptural conventions were changing during the first years of the reign of Darius. On the one hand we know that Darius was never again shown with a 'frontal' beard when depicted in a profile pose and on the other hand it is evident that this was just the moment when the representation of straight hair in Persian sculpture was changing from the 'undulating horizontal ridge convention' to the kind of gently waved, vertical lines that appear (in an experimental form) immediately below the circlet on Darius' head. As to the nature of the considerations that in the end ruled out any attempt to introduce a more up-to-date profile beard (if this ever was a serious goal), it can only be surmised that technical problems ultimately weighed against any such far-reaching emendation of the king's image.

Finally, while it is striking that the eight arms of the disc that caps the crown of Ahuramazda offer a kind of counterpoint to the eight-rayed stars in Darius' band-like 'battle crown', it is nothing less than mystifying that Darius' two followers (as opposed to Darius himself) were each portrayed with the same type of rare and seemingly archaic type of lobed bracelet as that which is found on the wrists of Ahuramazda (Pl. 16).[10]

Textual and visual documentation of an Achaemenid Persian identity

As we have already had occasion to notice, the opening phrases of the Bisitun inscription were specifically designed to underscore Darius' ultimate descent from Achaemenes and, hence, his membership in an Achamenid family that had 'from long ago' known kingship. By the same token it was to Darius' obvious advantage to paint Cyrus, as soon as he could find an appropriate setting in which to do so, as an individual who had himself chosen to be known, his long and distinguished antecedents notwithstanding, as nothing more, nor less, than 'an

Achaemenid' (cf. especially Stronach 1990: 200ff.). Fittingly enough, the opportunity to pro-mulgate this message lay very much to hand, at the still unfinished site of Pasargadae.

For reasons that are not clear, Cyrus chose to leave his monuments without exegetical texts; and Darius, who had already discovered the combined power of the written word and the sculpted image, was quick to turn this fortuitous circumstance to his advantage. To begin with, he drew up a brief, effective protocol (known to archaeologists as the CMa inscription) that would say exactly what he wanted – and no more than that. Composed in the first person singular (presumably in order to convey the impression that Cyrus himself had been the author) the text read: 'I, Cyrus, the King, an Achaemenid'. Readers of the inscription would have supplied for themselves the further (implicit) message: namely, that Cyrus, the Achaemenid, had 'built (or founded) this structure'.

In strictly logical terms, the inscription should only have been engraved in the two cuneiform scripts (Elamite and Akkadian) that would have been available to Cyrus. In response to a quickening sense of Persian identity, however, it is understandable that Darius chose to render the inscription in Old Persian as well – and that the two Old Persian lines were then given pride of place (Col. Pl. VI) in each of the buildings, Gate R, Palace S and Palace P, that came to be so labelled.[11]

The concept of a single seamless Achaemenid past was of course fortified in numerous other ways, most notably by the marriages that Darius contracted with each of the two surviving daughters of Cyrus (Herodotus III.88). But with a sure sense of the need for a permanent *visual* as well as a permanent textual affirmation of the harmonious nature of his 'succession', Darius took care to provide a series of bas-reliefs that would not only honour Cyrus but would, at the same time, also help to link this earlier monarch (and his sometimes jarringly archaic apotropaic sculptures) with the spirit – and the details – of his own newly evolving iconography of kingship. To this end, steps were taken to complete the unfinished fabric of Palace P in such a way that sculpted, mirror images of Cyrus (Col. Pl. VII) and an attendant would flank each of the two main doorways. Originally replete with innovative gold insets (but otherwise close in character to the style of sculpture that was soon to come to full maturity at Persepolis), each figure of Cyrus was also labelled, in the third person, as 'Cyrus, the Great King, an Achaemenid' (Kent 1953: CMc, 116); and, in one further text – Kent's CMb text – Darius appears (as far as the meaning of this last fragmentary inscription can be guessed at) to have duly made reference to his own part in this singular enterprise (Stronach 1978: 97ff.).

Conclusion

It is not always easy to re-examine the verities of a supposedly 'well known' period. Few episodes in history are more compelling, however, than those that are associated with the careers of Cyrus and Darius and, where such towering individuals are concerned, it is neces-sarily a matter for gratification if even just a few of the 'missing pieces of the puzzle' begin to look as if they might stand ready – at long last – to be nudged into place. In this broad context I think it is inescapable that Cyrus' line was an autochthonous one, still to some extent rooted in its Anshanite/Elamite past, even if it became more and more Persianised with the passage of time. Perhaps this was a balancing act that held almost no contradictions in the hands of someone of the exceptional stature of Cyrus. Equally, it may have been an exercise in state-craft and day-to-day governance that was somewhat beyond Cyrus' son and successor, the less assured, reportedly erratic Cambyses. At all events, the changes that Darius introduced when he came to the throne were probably far more drastic than has hitherto been realised. These still call for a more rigorous review than has been possible on this occasion, but it may not be too much to say that many basic questions, concerning such matters as the definition of a Persian identity, a Persian homeland, and even the nature of Persian religion, came to be reviewed and revised.

EPILOGUE
The fourfold garden at Pasargadae

Pasargadae was never a capital city in the traditional Near Eastern mould. At no time were its approaches fortified and, remarkably enough, its distinctive, freestanding buildings stood within the limits of a single, well-furnished royal park or 'paradise'.

In this agreeable ambience, directly adjacent to Palace P, Cyrus chose to lay out a formal Royal Garden (Fig. 21), the outlines of which are still indicated by a number of surviving stone watercourses and basins as well as by the foundations of two small garden pavilions (Col. Pl. VIII). This principal garden, which is at once distinguished by its numerous stone appointments, occupies a rectangular space c. 230 x 200 m in area; its corners, like those of the adjacent main buildings, are oriented towards the cardinal points of the compass; and the intended main focus of attention appears to have been a central, rectangular area which clearly took its longitudinal alignment from the cross-axis of Palace P.

The once-gleaming white stone water channels – built to last in the best Achaemenid tradi-tion – can be seen to have been 25 cm in width. They were punctuated at each corner, and otherwise at 13–14 m intervals, by deep square basins each c. 80 x 80 cm in size (Pl. 19). One further refinement consisted of the provision of a number of small stone sluice gates that were encountered on the north-east side of the central rectangle. These miniature gates were pre-sumably intended to divert water into earth channels that ran off at right angles in order to irrigate the adjacent trees and shrubs.

With reference to the new, practical disposition of garden space that can be noted in this plan, it is of interest to observe that the two small pavilions (Pavilions A and B) not only stand roughly opposite each other at some distance from Palace P, but that they also stand in approximately the same position as many later 'gate pavilions' in gardens of Islamic date. Indeed, the not quite precisely matched positions of the two pavilions might be counted as a mark of a still formative, as opposed to a fully mature, garden design.

Even Palace P as a whole could be said to represent a kind of 'ultimate garden pavilion' in that a permanent stone bench ran the whole length of the building's long south-east portico with, at the mid-point, a raised and enlarged stone foundation for an otherwise unique exter-

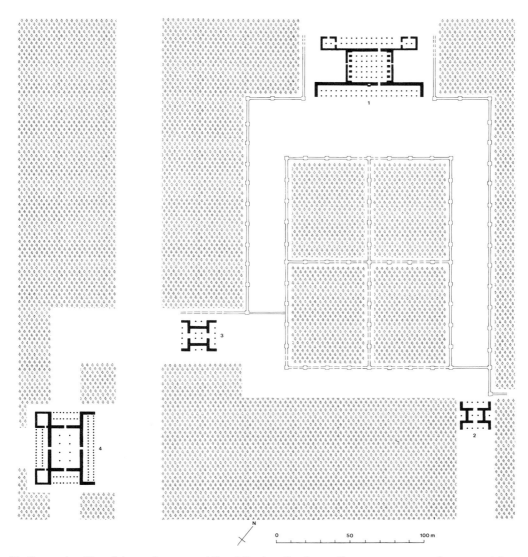

21 Pasargadae. Plan of the partly excavated Royal Garden. Continuous lines represent attested stone conduits; dashed lines represent postulated conduits. Numbered features include (1) Palace P; (2) Pavilion A; (3) Pavilion B; and (4) Palace S.

nal throne-seat (Stronach 1978: pl. 84). With excavated evidence from seventh/sixth century BC Media in mind, this later feature can be closely compared to the 'seat of honour' in the main hall of the Godin II citadel (Young and Levine 1974: fig. 37). The difference, of course, is that Cyrus took the fixed throne-seat and continuous internal bench of a traditional Median columned hall and transposed these same features to a shaded but nonetheless *outdoor* setting at his more southerly capital. Thus, at suitable seasons of the year, Cyrus appears to have intended to use his garden as a backdrop for his audiences, i.e. as a place where his gaze might lift, not to the columns of a standard reception hall, but to the prospect (let us say) of cypress trees and roses – and brimming water channels.

On a more personal note, I was originally under the impression (when I was excavating at Pasargadae in the early 1960s) that the structure of the central portion of the royal garden could only be reconstructed through the presence of one or another well-attested stone conduits. On these grounds I came to the conclusion – on the basis of an admittedly limited amount of excavation – that the path-surrounded central space had originally consisted of two contiguous rectangular plots that had stood parallel, in their longest dimension, to the south-east facade of Palace P. The solution was not overly elegant, but at the time I was not aware of any good reason to fault it.

There matters rested until the late 1980s when an improbable reconstruction of the garden drew my attention to a missing component in the plan. In line with Lysander's description of Cyrus the Younger's late fifth-century BC park or 'paradise' located near Sardis (*Oiconomicus* 4. 20ff.), in which the trees were said to have been planted in straight lines in a design that was 'exact and arranged at right angles', I had taken care to ask a draughtsman (who was at the time working on a reconstruction of the Palace Area at Pasargadae) to be sure to include straight, parallel rows of trees running perpendicular to the south-east portico of Palace P. But when the finished drawing reached me, I was disconcerted to find that one such file of trees had been placed *directly in line* with Cyrus' fixed throne-seat. Only then did I realise that, whether or not an additional stone water channel had ever graced the long axis of the garden – an issue that can only be resolved through the agency of further excavation – Cyrus would undoubtedly have planned to enjoy an uninterrupted vista down the long axis of his outdoor sanctum.

When such a 'vista of power' is identified as an integral part of the design, a very different plan is manifested. The central portion of the garden suddenly falls into four plots: a quadripartite design that is, I submit, wholly consistent with the rhythmic proportions of the available space as a whole (Fig. 21). Thus, Cyrus almost certainly deserves to be credited with the first known introduction of a *chahar bagh* or 'fourfold garden', a configuration that has remained a permanent canon in Persian garden design. Indeed, even if Cyrus was not the inventor of such a concept, which accords so well with the innate sense of balance in Persian taste (not to mention his claim to be 'king of the four quarters'), it seems more than likely that his known association with such a practical and appealing design did much to make the fourfold garden a symbol for rightful rule, both while his own memory still survived and even long afterwards. Thus it is that gardens of this stamp not only seem to have stood as a mark of legitimate authority in Sasanian and later Iran, but also in times and places yet further removed from early south-west Iran: from the fourteenth-century AD Lion Court of the Alhambra in southern Spain to the great gardens of Mughal India (Stronach 1994: 8ff.).

By a strange quirk of fate Darius himself may also have played a role in rescuing Cyrus' innovative design from possible oblivion. That is to say that, but for his decision to complete the construction of the Palace P, and to carry out still other related works in the adjacent area of the Royal Garden,[12] knowledge of this sixth-century BC *chahar bagh* might not have survived. As it is, the mid fourth-century BC date of some of the exquisite Achaemenid gold jewellery (Col. Pls IX–X) that came to be hidden in a humble water jar directly beside one of the porticoes of Pavilion B (Stronach 1978: 168ff.) offers a strong indication that the Royal Garden at Pasargadae continued to flourish down to the last days of Achaemenid dominion.

Notes

1 A contingent of troops, identified as originating in 'Parsuash' was included in the Elamite-led forces that opposed Sennacherib at the battle of Halule in northern Babylonia in 691 BC. Interestingly enough, this is the last time that the Assyrians refer to Persians as part of a hostile Elamite coalition. Zadok suggests (1991: 236) that the Persians were present as 'allies' of the Elamites, but an alternative view that they were, at this time, merely conscripted vassals of Elam (Brentjes 1995: 1014) is, I think, more persuasive.

2 Thus Cyrus is referred to as 'king of the country of Anshan' *c.* 550 BC, and as 'king of the country of Parsa' some three years later.

3 For the final publication of the figural image of the Persepolis seal (PFS 93) and its inscription, see Garrison and Root forthcoming.

4 For a contrary interpretation, however, note also Miroschedji 1985: 276.

5 Apparently the latter form of the name would have been 'easier for speakers of Persian'. I am indebted to Professor Martin Schwartz for this observation.

6 In a more comprehensive scheme extending down to 330 BC, Mature Achaemenid art (which could very well also be defined as 'Middle Achaemenid art') could be said to give way to 'Later Achaemenid art' somewhere within, say, the third quarter of the fifth century BC.

7 Another very special achievement of Cyrus was to dare to set so much space between his separate monuments. It should be remembered, however, that the Medes had already shown a predilection for separate, discrete structures, even within the limits, as at Tepe Nush-i Jan, of strictly finite, enclosed space (cf. Stronach and Roaf 1978: fig. 1).

8 New support for this contention appears to come from certain recent, clandestine excavations in N.W. Iran (cf. Mousavi 1994; Curtis 1995: 20). Elsewhere, a limestone plaque of Neo-Elamite date from Susa (Pl. 15) has long demonstrated just how willing the Elamites themselves were to borrow Neo-Assyrian apotropaic imagery. In this case, however, the figures of the smiting god and the lion-demon are not close copies of the original Assyrian models (Harper *et al.*, 1992: 201) and the Elamite sculptor has misunderstood, for example, the nature of the Assyrian short kilt with its long, pendant fringe.

9 It remains notoriously difficult to make sense of the religious situation at this period. In line with the fact that Ahuramazda appears to be worshipped as a supreme god, but not necessarily within a Zoroastrian context (cf. Frye 1962: 94), it has recently been suggested (Sancisi-Weerdenburg 1995: 1042) that the prevailing local belief in western Iran in the late sixth century BC might be best referred to (at least in neutral terms) as 'Mazdaism'.

10 Whether or not the accession of Darius marks a moment of religious change in western Iran remains obscure. The fact that Darius chose to make no further use of such non-Iranian images as 'the smiting god', that he allowed himself to refer to certain Elamites as 'faithless' in the latest section of the Bisitun inscription (Kent 1953: 134), and that he saw fit to describe Gaumata (an individual who, at the very least, assumed the identity of Bardiya) as 'a Magian' (Kent 1953: 120), could each point to the emergence of a degree of difference (a new, more Persian degree of emphasis perhaps) between his own religious tenets and those of Cyrus. On the other hand, Darius' repeated reference to the all-important 'favour' of Ahuramazda strongly suggests that this same deity already occupied a significant, very possibly pre-eminent position for some time before Darius launched his bid for power.

11 One of the clearest proofs that the Old Persian script was invented under Darius, not Cyrus, resides – paradoxically – in the wording of the CMa text. Had this 'first person text' been his own, Cyrus would undoubtedly have elected to include his father's name. Conversely, it is fair to say that Darius would have had no interest in spelling out Cyrus' immediate genealogy and every interest in proclaiming the latter's putative, distant link with Achaemenes. See also Stronach, forthcoming.

12 Marks of a standard-sized toothed chisel (a stone working tool that only came into use in Iran some years after the death of Cyrus) are clearly visible on the surface of several of the stone blocks that went into the construction of one part of one conduit on the south-west side of the garden.

Susa under Achaemenid Rule

Institut Français de Recherche en Iran

Introduction

The ancient Greek writers were familiar with Susa, which was regarded as a capital of the Achamenid empire, but hardly knew of Persepolis. Impressed by the royal road, Herodotus (V. 52–3) and Xenophon (*Cyropaedia* VIII.6, 17–18) describe the itinerary from Sardis to Susa via Babylon, but go no further. In *The Persians* by Aeschylus, the news of the defeat of the Great King was carried to Susa. Later, in the time of Xerxes, it is in Susa that the story of Esther is set (Esther 1:2). During the conquest of Alexander, Susa was taken a few months before Persepolis and this event made a strong impression even upon Alexander who returned there to celebrate his conquest of the empire. Later writers (Strabo, Diodorus Siculus) mention and sometimes describe Susa, but never Persepolis.

In recent times, however, archaeologists have marvelled at the grandiose ruins of Persepolis, as do today's visitors, whereas Susa is thought of rather as a multi-period city where the Achaemenid settlement is just one in a series of levels with important ruins. The respective roles of the two capitals are, then, subjects for discussion. It is especially ironic that Susa, considered to be the administrative capital, has produced only a handful of inscribed tablets and foundation stones, whereas Persepolis has produced thousands of tablets dealing with administrative and economic affairs, although admittedly they primarily concern the city and its region. In this paper I would like to review the Achaemenid remains at Susa, which are essentially limited to the palace, then discuss the absence of evidence which would indicate a capital. Finally, by offering some explanation for this lack of evidence, I will propose the hypothesis that Susa was a relatively empty capital, before and even during the Achaemenid period.

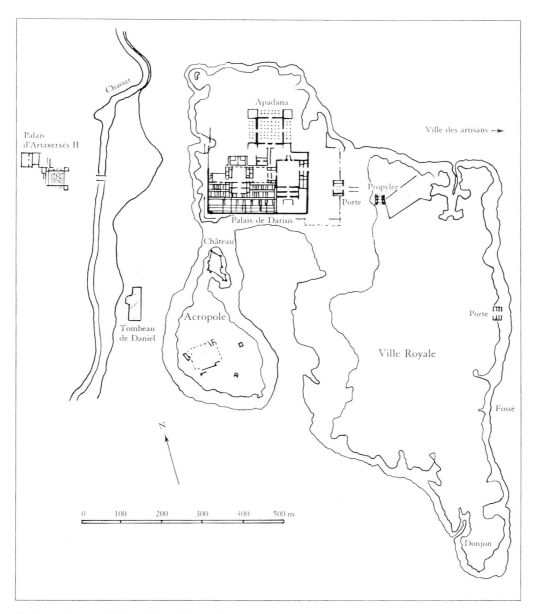

22 Map of the Royal City of Susa in the Achaemenid period.

From the time when Shush, in the province of Khuzistan in south-western Iran, was identified as Biblical Shushan and the Susa of antiquity, nineteenth-century scholars turned their attention to the Achaemenid audience palace, the Apadana, which they discovered easily through the remains of capitals and column bases (Loftus 1857: 366 ff; see now Curtis 1993). In 1851–2, Colonel W.F. Williams and William K. Loftus, then the latter alone, both appointed by the Turco-Persian Frontier Commission, were able to locate these elements, to draw up even then a correct plan of the Apadana, the columned hall, and to record the trilingual royal inscriptions (see a summary of this expedition in Curtis 1993: 1–15, pls 1b, 3–12, showing some examples of the plans and drawings by Henry A. Churchill who worked with Loftus). These were the first images of Susa known to the public in the west (Pl. 20). Between 1884 and 1886, the French expedition of the Dieulafoys revealed this impressive architecture to the general public; it became known through their books (J. Dieulafoy 1888; M. Dieulafoy 1893) and the creation of a special hall in the Louvre, containing in particular a column with its base and capital (Pl. 22) as well as wall friezes of glazed bricks. Beyond the palace, M. Dieulafoy found elements of the city walls of which he made a very complicated and fanciful reconstruction. Apart from the palace of Darius little was known, although W.K. Loftus had indicated the existence of Achaemenid and Greek remains at the opposite end of the city (Fig. 22, 'Donjon').

Following the creation of the Délégation Archéologique Française en Perse in 1897, all the directors took an interest in the Achaemenid palace, with varying degrees of success. The first director, J. de Morgan, was a prehistorian; he entrusted to M. Pillet, an architect, the task of uncovering the ruins of the palace and attempting a reconstruction, which he did in a plan and in watercolours (Col. Pls XI–XII; Pillet 1914). Between 1920 and 1969, the two successive directors of the expedition, R. De Mecquenem and R. Ghirshman, continued to take an interest in the palace of Darius, but were to change little our vision of the city and the palace. This was left to Jean Perrot, the last excavator of Susa. Between 1969 and 1978 he went through the notes of his predecessors, verifying the details of what remained after so much excavation, and he brought to light unsuspected monuments of which the most remarkable was the statue of Darius (Kervran et al. 1972; Perrot 1981).

The Achaemenid city of Susa is better known today, but difficult to appreciate on the ground. For the visitor arriving at the royal city of Susa, the first impression is very disappointing. Even from the top of the highest mound, the Acropolis, one can only see the sparse remains covering the area of the so-called Apadana mound, which corresponds to the palace of Darius; here most of the visible remains – mud brick walls, stone fragments of capitals and columns – have been partially restored by the excavators. Apart from this area, it is difficult to distinguish any other Achaemenid ruins, either on the eastern tell, the Ville Royale, facing the Apadana, or those situated on the west bank of the Shaur river.

In no way can the Achaemenid remains of Susa be compared with Persepolis, where some standing structures reach 20 m, nearly the level of the roof, and the whole terrace gives an impression of numerous columned halls and walls partly built with worked stone. In Susa, the highest preserved stone structures attain a maximum of 2 m, and the visible remains cover barely 15 hectares, although it is known that the royal city extended over 100 hectares.

As far as we know, Cyrus the Great did not carry out any building work in Susa, and it was only after the beginning of Darius' reign that the old Elamite city underwent a transformation. In fact, the seizure of Susa by Cyrus is not recorded; this event apparently took place around

539 BC, when Cyrus was en route to Babylon. The fact that it was not mentioned is significant, as it probably indicates that Susa was no longer a major political centre at this time.

Probably early in the reign of Darius, about 519 BC, and before he began to build in Persepolis, he chose Susa as one of his capitals (Steve 1974: 27, Vallat 1986: 281). Within a few decades, the city was completely remodelled and replanned. Darius' architects took into account the three archaeological tells, which rose to different heights after some thirty-five centuries of occupation. They decided that the lozenge formed by the Apadana, the Acropolis and the Ville Royale (as they were labelled by the first French excavators) would form the basis for the royal city. They levelled some areas and filled in others to create a level surface 15 m above the water level of the Shaur river, except in the central part. This area of 100 hectares was defined by an almost vertical glacis, not by a curtain-wall. The most recent excavations have made it clear that the royal city was not fortified,[1] which tells us a lot about the vision the Great King had of his empire and the impression he wished to make upon his subjects.

Within this perimeter (Fig. 22), the small valley between the Apadana and the Ville Royale was deepened and the slopes cut to create steep faces in order to isolate the royal palace and render it more impressive. For this important building a very sophisticated system of foundations was devised, more than 10 m deep, to support the columns and the walls. The replanning of the site was so profound and durable that it was still visible when the first excavators located the palace of Darius and correctly named the different areas (Loftus 1857: fig. 314; Curtis 1993: fig. 1).

The Achaemenid remains in the northern zone (Fig. 22)

The known remains are concentrated in the north and north-west parts of the lozenge, and this distribution is one of the things which has to be explained.[2] The only entrance found so far, a monumental gate, stands alone on the eastern slope of the Ville Royale. Then there is a large gap in our knowledge extending to the so-called Propylaeum more than 500 m to the west.[3] The Propylaeum is a small square mud brick building, 24 m x 24 m, which comprises two oblong rooms decorated with recesses, between two small porticoes. Its stone column bases each consist of two stepped square plinths, typical of Achaemenid architecture. This mud brick building, discovered in the mid-1970s, was badly damaged by the construction of later Parthian houses and is hardly visible today (Fig. 22, restored plan).

To the west lies Darius' palace which, although it has no façade, has an isolated monumental gate. Access is via a bridge, 30 m long, which stretches across the deep ditch. This architectural complex covers some 13 hectares (Figs. 23, 24). The gate, 40 m x 28 m, is a tall structure and is very similar to the gate of Xerxes at Persepolis. Both are examples of an Achaemenid innovation which has no connection with Mesopotamian architecture. The main room has four square column bases and a trilingual inscription by Xerxes, announcing the completion of the building begun by his father Darius (Vallat 1974). It is after walking through this kind of triumphal arch and turning around that the visitor would have seen the

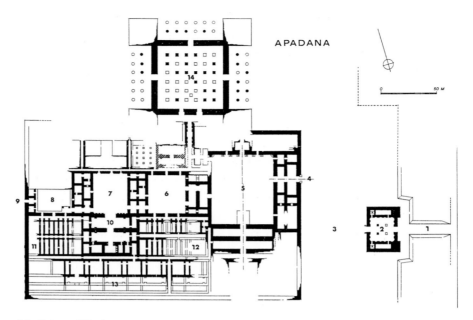

23 Plan of the Palace of Darius.

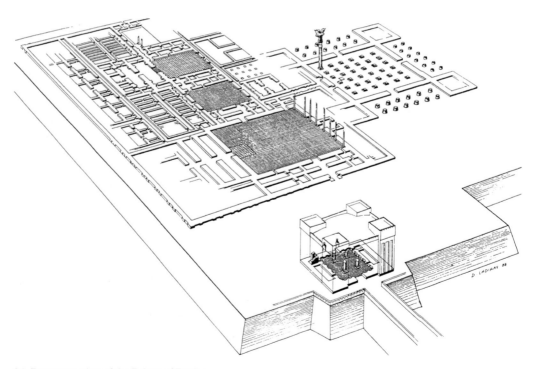

24 Reconstruction of the Palace of Darius.

famous statue of Darius, against one of the door jambs (Fig. 25, Pl. 21). Found in 1972, this larger than life-size sculpture was about 3.50 m high with its base when it was complete; the upper third is now missing. Represented in an Egyptianising pose, the king wears Persian dress (Stronach 1974a) which bears a trilingual cuneiform inscription and a hieroglyphic inscription announcing: 'This is Darius the king who ordered this statue to be made in Egypt', originally for a temple at Heliopolis (Vallat 1974). Chemical analysis has confirmed that the grey limestone is not from the Zagros mountains, but from Wadi Hammamat in eastern Egypt. The top and three sides of the base, measuring 1.04 m x 0.64 m, bear other hieroglyphic inscriptions and cartouches depicting the twenty-four peoples of the empire (Roaf 1974). Judging from some sculptured fragments on the same scale previously found in excavations, apparently all on the Apadana, the gate could have had two or four royal statues (Luschey 1983).

On the west side of the Darius gate is an open area without any construction. The visitor would have faced the palace itself, not to be entered, and turning right could have approached the audience hall, the tallest building in the complex. The Apadana, so called by Darius himself, is a huge pillared hall 58 m square and about 20 m high. It was recognised as early as 1852 by Loftus (1857: fig. p. 366; Curtis 1993: fig. 2). The six rows of six square plinths supported fluted stone columns and composite capitals which, like those of the Apadana at Persepolis, have Persian, Egyptian, Syrian and Ionian components (Pls 20, 22). A stone foundation for a throne is still visible in the middle of the northern row. On three sides, the central hall is surrounded by porticoes with two rows of six columns resting on bell-shaped bases. As a whole the Apadana is a square, with each side measuring 109 m, quite similar in many respects to that of Persepolis. The only striking difference is the absence of a terrace at Susa. Thus, a staircase and the associated decoration which is so distinctive at Persepolis could not have existed here. Therefore, none of the famous long glazed brick friezes found in the early excavations at Susa could have been in such a position, as has sometimes been assumed.

The palace itself, which covers 5 hectares, is a huge rectangle (246 m x 155 m), generally organised around three main courtyards (Figs 23, 24). The western courtyard gives access to the royal apartments, which contain the two largest rooms; between these rooms, beneath the jambs of the door, two copies of the foundation charter were found in 1970, one in Akadian, the other in Elamite. A copy in Old Persian had previously been found nearby (Vallat 1970 and 1986). They all confirm that the building was the work of Darius and explain how the various peoples of the empire contributed to it, bringing the materials or working them. In the eastern courtyard, which is the largest, the famous frieze of glazed bricks depicting lions was discovered fallen on the floor, while in the western part, pieces of the

25 The statue of Darius that stood against the western door of the gate to his palace.

frieze showing life-sized guards or archers were scattered in the debris (Col. Pl. XIII; Amiet 1988: fig. 81; Harper *et al.* 1992: nos. 155–69).

The structure is clearly dated to the late sixth century BC and was completed by Xerxes, as he himself claimed. Some parts were later rebuilt by Artaxerxes II in the early fourth century, after fire had destroyed it in the mid-fifth century. For both periods of construction, the royal palace, taken as a whole, is a remarkable illustration of Achaemenid art and architecture, whose diversity of origins is defined today as 'positive eclecticism' (Nylander 1979: 355; Root 1979: 15–16, 24). The hypostyle audience hall is Iranian in architecture and plan, known some decades before at Pasargadae in a rectangular plan, and originating even earlier in the architecture of north-western and western Iran in the Iron Age and in the Median period (short summary in Roaf 1995: 65). However, the supports and their elements come from outside Iran (see above). Conversely, the plan of the palace evokes certain Mesopotamian models, both of the Neo-Assyrian period as at Nineveh, and above all of the Neo-Babylonian period, such as the palace of Nebuchadnezzar at Babylon (Amiet 1974: 65–7, fig. 2) or his summer palace (Calmeyer 1994: 143–5, figs 3–4). One finds here structures arranged around a series of courtyards, and in each case there are great halls in a row, laid out lengthwise, communicating through the long sides. The same Mesopotamian influence may also be found in the friezes of polychrome glazed bricks, which evoke those of the Ishtar gate at Babylon, some decades older. However, from the end of the second millennium BC onwards, the Elamites and then the Neo-Elamites of Susa knew how to decorate the walls of temples and palaces with baked bricks in relief (Amiet 1988: figs. 62–3).

Other buildings within and outside the city

Despite the impressive size of the royal complex it contains only a palace, although some classical writers (namely Strabo XV.3.21) inform us that every Persian king built a residence, a treasury and a series of storerooms. In fact, the fragmentary cuneiform inscriptions scattered around the site indicate that there were other buildings (Steve 1987: 96, n. 228; Harper *et al.* 1992: 216). Can these be identified?

The so-called Donjon palace, at the very southern end of the Ville Royale, could have played a role, if it is an Achaemenid construction. Its date and function are still debated. It has not survived in elevation and the layout is rather enigmatic. The plan is hardly visible in the restored walls resting in narrow foundation trenches. In the debris several carved orthostats have been found, the only examples so far discovered within the city. They represent servants at half life-size, several of them climbing stairs. Various small bell-shaped bases have also been found, as well as two square plinths and some Aramaic graffiti of the Persian period. In the vicinity a well has yielded numerous ivory pieces clearly datable to the Achaemenid period (Amiet 1972). Thus there are several indications of an Achaemenid occupation, particularly evidenced by building techniques and decoration, but other factors contradict such a date and indicate a re-use of Achaemenid elements (of unknown origin): (1) the gravel foundations are very narrow in comparison with actual Achaemenid ones; (2) one of the square plinths discovered by Loftus bears a Greek inscription engraved upside down (late third/second century BC) and is made of an unusual white limestone; (3) R. de Mecquenem, the excavator, found many fragments of Hellenising figurines, which may be dated to the Seleucid and early Parthian periods, mixed in with the foundations; (4) a number of Seleucid coins have been found, including a small coin hoard of Alexander type dating to about 300 BC; their precise find-spots are not clear, but some were apparently found in the foundations. Thus the hypothesis of an original Achaemenid building here cannot be dismissed (Amiet 1988: 133–4), but very probably the present building is wholly or partly of the later Seleucid or Parthian periods (Stronach 1985a: 434–5; Boucharlat 1990a: 150–1).

As for other remains of the Achaemenid period within the city, there is a single wall of this date on the Ville Royale identified by the pottery associated with it. Obviously this was an irregularly settled domestic area without any official character. There are also some traces of the Achaemenid period on the outskirts of the royal city, namely on the very large tell called the Artisans Quarter, whose surface area is equal to that of the three others combined. But in spite of the fact that there is no evidence of earlier periods here, there are only few remains of the Achaemenid period. All that we need to consider is the so-called 'village perse achéménide', excavated in the early 1950s by R. Ghirshman (1954). This consists of a series of rooms dating from the sixth century BC which were reoccupied during the Achaemenid period, according to the pottery and a single cuneiform tablet of the early fourth century BC.

More official buildings are situated on the other side of the Shaur river, about 350 m west of the Apadana, where a palace of Artaxerxes II, smaller than that of Darius, was discovered in 1969 and subsequently excavated (Labrousse and Boucharlat 1972; Boucharlat and Labrousse 1979). This *tachara*, as it is called in a cuneiform (Akkadian and Elamite) inscription on a stone plinth found amongst the debris, or *hadish*[4] in the Old Persian form (Vallat 1979), covered some 3 hectares but only a quarter is preserved (Pl. 23). The most distinctive area is a hypostyle hall (37.50 m x 34.60 m) with eight rows of eight bell-shaped column bases; the columns themselves were of wood rather than stone. The painted decoration has partly survived and is our first evidence for wall decoration. It is in blue (cobalt), red (iron oxide and cinnabar), white and black, and also covered the shafts and column bases. On the walls people in local dress are depicted within a framework of floral and geometric motifs (Col. Pls XIV–XV).

In the rest of the complex, only the raised Building III is worthy of mention. The plan can be reconstructed from the layout of the foundations on a terrace 2.50 m high. These consist of a grid of mud-brick walls defining areas filled with gravel (Fig. 26). There is a square central room which probably had four columns, with narrow rooms on three sides. On the fourth side the main portico opens on to the garden. A smaller portico on the east opens on to a courtyard. In this area decoration has been found, including some stone orthostats showing servants climbing a staircase, as in the Donjon area (Col. Pl. XVI), and numerous fragments of glazed bricks without relief. We cannot prove that these two types of decoration actually come from this palace, but it should be noted that this raised Building III would have required a

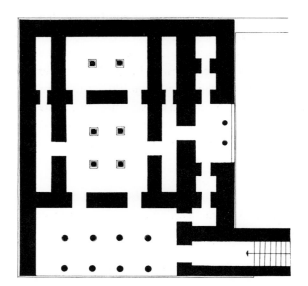

26 Reconstructed plan of Building III in the Shaur Palace.

staircase. The palace of Artaxerxes is dated to the beginning of the fourth century (with Building III being a later addition) but its function is not clear. Did Artaxerxes build it as a residence which would be more private than the palace of Darius? Or did he construct it as a temporary residence while the Apadana was being rebuilt after destruction by fire? If so, where did his father and grandfather live after the Apadana was burnt in the mid-fifth century BC?

The date and function of the last building to be considered, the Ayadana, are obscure. The few remains, located 4 km north of the Apadana, were excavated in the late nineteenth century by Dieulafoy, but unfortunately they have since been completely levelled (Dieulafoy 1893: 411–6). The Ayadana consists of two terraces, the largest (36 m x 26 m) supporting a courtyard surrounded by narrow corridors; the second terrace (28 m x 21.60 m), slightly higher, contains a square room, or *cella*, 10 m each side, with four bell-shaped stone column bases. In the centre is an altar restored by Dieulafoy. This central room is surrounded by narrow rooms and a portico with two columns opening on to the main courtyard. The building techniques all point to an Achaemenid construction – gravel foundations, terraces, the size of the rooms, foot and cubit units, bell-shaped column bases, and the plan of the main area, which is similar to the plan of some constructions at Persepolis and to Building III of the Shaur palace. Dieulafoy thus considered it to be an Achaemenid building, of religious significance because of some nude female figurines he found there. He labelled it the Ayadana, 'house of gods', and this building has been regarded as the prototype of the Iranian fire temple for almost a century. In examining this building, Ghirshman (1976: 197–200) demonstrated that the column bases in the *cella* were re-used stones. Then Stronach (1985b: 620–2) after careful examination came to the conclusion that the column bases came from different sources, thus confirming a post-Achaemenid re-use. At the same time H.-P. Francfort (1977:

279–80) has pointed out that the plan of this building is similar to several Graeco-Bactrian domestic houses in northern Afghanistan and southern Turkmenistan (third–second centuries BC). As far as we know, there is no object illustrated by Dieulafoy which can be securely dated to the Achaemenid period, and the figurines which he attributes to the goddess Anahita are certainly post-Achaemenid, as hundreds of them are known elsewhere in Susa. In conclusion, the Ayadana cannot be completely ruled out as an Achaemenid construction, but it is more likely to be a post-Achaemenid residence, built with re-used Achaemenid architectural elements as the Sassanian inhabitants were to do some centuries later (Ghirshman 1976: 200; Boucharlat 1990b: 230–31).

The missing evidence

Having considered the certain or possible remains of the Achaemenid period at Susa, we should now draw attention to the absence of evidence:

1 Considering the whole area of the royal city (100 hectares) and its surroundings, the surviving Achaemenid structures are few and concentrated in one part in the north, covering some 15 per cent of the city.

2 The absence of a citadel, if it existed, as well as garrison quarters. Although the upper levels of the Acropolis mound were explored too hastily, the excavators would surely have noticed the impressive walls belonging to such a citadel. Apart from a brief mention of the city wall, nothing can be found in the excavation reports, nor are there any convincing descriptions in the classical sources (Boucharlat 1990b: 226).

3 The absence of temples. This has been explained by what we know of the Iranian religion through the ancient authors. According to Herodotus (I.141), the Persians had no temples, no idols, no altars, and no permanent religious structures. None of the Greek authors mention any building which might correspond to a temple, and for them this rarity of religious buildings in Persia must have been striking.

4 The absence of cemeteries. This can hardly be explained by the religious customs of this period: if the Achaemenids were adherents of Zoroastrianism, one could expect, in the absence of graves, at least evidence of secondary burials, as mentioned in much later texts. And there are the very fine examples of royal tombs at Persepolis and Naqsh-i Rustam. At Susa the only known tombs are two bath-tub coffins made of bronze, found in a vaulted tomb on the Acropolis (Col. Pl. XVII). One was empty, while the other contained a rich collection of jewellery arranged around the skeleton (de Morgan 1905; Harper *et al.* 1992: 242–52). It is dated by Syro-Phoenician coins found in the coffin to the very end of the Achaemenid period, i.e. after 350 BC (Elayi and Elayi 1992).

5 The lack of written evidence. We have a serious problem in that the archives have never been recovered at Susa. Five contracts in Akkadian and some dated tablets from Susa

found on the site and elsewhere (Stolper 1992) cannot be compared with the thousands of tablets found at Persepolis. Although the latter mainly concern regional administration and cover a rather short period, they do nevertheless exist. Apart from these few tablets, the written evidence at Susa is restricted to the series of inscriptions on column bases mentioned above and the official foundation charters, often reproduced on clay tablets, clay barrel cylinders and sometimes on the glazed brick friezes (Steve 1987; Vallat 1970, 1974, 1979, 1986).

6 The objects which can be dated to the Achaemenid period are so few that it has long been almost impossible to define the material culture of this period.[5] The beautiful collection of ivories that we have already mentioned, many of them imported from Egypt, Phoenicia and Asia Minor, is the most distinctive contribution (Amiet 1972). Other random discoveries, such as two bronze weights (Harper *et al.* 1992: no. 154), ivory combs, and the jewellery from the only grave, complete our information.

Looking for Achaemenid Susa

To explain the paucity of remains, a series of questions needs to be asked:

1 Are we mistaken about the chronology of the earlier or later remains and therefore the series of objects which might actually be attributed to the Achaemenid period?

2 Can we hope to discover new buildings by excavating in other parts of the site, either inside or outside the city?

3 Have part of the remains, large or small, been destroyed by later occupation – the site was occupied down to the Mongol period – as occurred in the palace of Darius?

4 Finally, does what we know actually represent all that remains from the Achaemenid empire?

1   The question of chronology

Until the 1970s, the internal chronology of Susa in the first millennium BC was not defined because these 'late periods' had not received much attention. Thanks to recent research, the stratigraphy and chronology are now much better known. There is a corpus of domestic pottery for the pre-Achaemenid period, for the Achaemenid period itself, and for the following centuries. Pottery of the Achaemenid period has actually been found in only one area of the Ville Royale, and it is definitely very rare elsewhere. The first excavators did not pay much attention to these modest remains, although they kept a good deal of pottery from other 'late periods', especially from the Seleucid and Parthian, even presenting short reports about the post-Achaemenid structures, but they did not do the same for the Achaemenid period. Therefore there is far less material from the Achaemenid period than from others. Finally, the absence of precious objects is not particularly surprising in a city which was occupied for many centuries afterwards: such objects would have been stolen, carried away or melted down.

2   The search for other buildings

Despite the large and numerous trenches dug at Susa since 1851, large parts of the site still remain untouched (Ghirshman 1954: plan 1; Boucharlat 1985: fig. 1). However, there is no hope of discovering more about the Achaemenid period in the Acropolis, which is today excavated down to the third-millennium levels, nor in the Apadana which is also almost fully excavated. In the Ville Royale, the large trenches dug over the course of a century are unpromising. The negative results of the archaeomagnetic survey show that there is little chance of discovering important buildings in this tell: we may expect only more scattered domestic structures of the type already produced in the excavations.

On the Artisans tell, which is outside the limits of the royal city, the numerous trial trenches indicate that this 100-hectare area was generally only settled from post-Achaemenid times onwards and was mainly occupied by cemeteries and workshops until the Islamic period. Finally, around the four tells, growing urbanisation in the last thirty years has not brought to light many remains. For the Achaemenid period onwards, only a stone staircase is worthy of mention: the series of five steps indicates Achaemenid work, but the context is dated to Parthian times (Boucharlat and Shahidi 1987).

3   The destruction of the Achaemenid city

The hypothesis of destruction, intentional during the conquest of Alexander or accidental during later occupations, seems to be the best answer to our question, but does not work very well. Taking the palace of Darius as an example, it is clear that Alexander and his followers did not destroy Susa as they did Persepolis (Boucharlat 1990b). It is likely that the huge structures of the Apadana fell down within a few decades for lack of maintenance. The palace itself was reoccupied, apparently by ordinary people who gradually converted the large rooms into small spaces as they did in the Shaur palace. From the Parthian period onwards new houses were built, re-using some Achaemenid materials such as pieces of stone, glazed bricks and even the statue of Darius. However, the Achaemenid buildings could still be found in these areas, even when re-used or covered with new structures. The Propylaeum was also seriously damaged by the construction of two successive large houses of the Parthian period, both of which have large, deep foundation trenches. Again, though, the plan and some parts of the Achaemenid building were found and are clearly recognisable.

The post-Achaemenid remains, and especially those of the Seleucid period, are of two types, those that re-used Achaemenid structures and completely new buildings. In the first case, the re-used structures did not completely hide their Achaemenid predecessors as official buildings were not re-used for official purposes. The only possible exception is the Donjon, where fragments of Greek architectural elements and a dozen Greek inscriptions mentioning public civil buildings and temples indicate an official post-Achaemenid building. On the other hand, large buildings with Hellenising decorative elements, mosaics, figurines and pottery occur frequently in the Ville Royale in an area which apparently contained no building during Achaemenid times.

4   The empty royal city

Although the discovery of remains in the future should not be ruled out, the conclusion must be that the city was not densely settled with permanent structures during Achaemenid times. It would seem that Achaemenid Susa was almost empty. Although we cannot exclude the existence of flimsy structures that have not survived, the idea emerges of a city which was sparsely built up or not permanently or densely occupied. The fact that the Achaemenid kings had several capitals is not a sufficient or satisfactory explanation. Persepolis possesses many buildings both on the terrace and at its foot, and in addition there are numerous isolated structures, partly in stone, scattered in the Marv Dasht plain. Moreover, Persepolis was apparently created *ex nihilo* as a capital by Darius, whereas Susa, though reduced in size in the first millennium BC, was still a town when Darius decided to build his palace there.

The hypothesis of a slow transformation of south-west Iran from the mid-second millennium onwards into a pastoral region with nomadic or semi-nomadic populations would explain the paucity of permanent housing (Perrot 1985). However, this could also be valid for the Persepolis area (Sumner 1986), which is much more densely built up. When Darius chose Susa as a capital, he may have expelled the local Elamite inhabitants, but there should be traces of them in Susiana; in fact, the Neo-Elamite or Neo-Elamite-derived settlements of the sixth to fifth centuries BC are not numerous in the Susiana plain (Wenke 1975–6).[6]

Finally, I would suggest that Susa had a very low density of settlement in the late sixth century BC. Darius' choice was dictated by the past prestige of the old city and the king had no difficulty in replanning it, as it had been only a small town for several decades or centuries and was partly ruined as he states in his inscriptions.

Such a hypothesis of a reduced population does not explain the apparent absence of the newcomers, the Persians, from the sixth century onwards. We can accept the idea of the Achaemenid army camping for a few months every year, as well as the craftsmen who built the royal buildings, but it seems hardly applicable to the court, which had to be housed, and the administration, which had to work and to store. Did the frequent moving of the court not affect thousands of people? Was the stay of the court at Susa not long enough during the year to justify many permanent buildings?[7]

In fact, although the classical writers referred to Susa as the imperial capital, we should not imagine it as a modern capital with numerous specialised, permanent buildings. The Great King spent a large part of the year not only going from one capital to another, but travelling slowly with many detours to meet his 'peoples' and tribes, to receive 'tribute' and offer gifts, etc. (Briant 1988). The king was accompanied by his guard, hundreds of servants, the court, and very likely an administrative staff plus numerous wagons for the equipment. These thousands of people lived in a well-organised camp, including a 'palais démontable' (with the horses' stables!) which was the centre of power (Briant 1988: 267–9). Apart from being a temporary royal capital, Susa was first of all the capital of the satrapy of Elam, as Persepolis was for Fars, attested by the thousands of tablets which deal with the administration of the city and the province.

The nomadism of the Great King was above all highly political, a way of governing, much more than journeys between the regions according to the season. It was necessary to visit the countryside regularly to show, and to remind his subjects of, the royal power. The royal camp must have been magnificent and well equipped to manage the empire while travelling. In these circumstances the fixed capitals of the Achaemenids did not have the importance which we attribute to modern capitals. If the constructions of Darius at Persepolis and at Susa are impressive, their role was more political than practical. The city of Susa, enclosing only the palace of Darius and a few other buildings, would thus have been less a true administrative centre of the empire than a magnificent empty showcase, used only from time to time.

Notes

1 A fortification wall, 27 m wide, is reported by R. Ghirshman (1965: 6, figs. 2 and 22–3) to the north of the Ville Royale and this has often been cited by other authors. Only the lower part of it has been found, capping an older Elamite wall. There is no indication that this wall stood above the Achaemenid ground level. Concerning the written evidence, one of Darius' inscriptions (DSe) tells us the king rebuilt the previous fortifications, Old Persian *dastakartam* (Steve 1974: 25–6), which were in ruins, but does not describe them. Later Strabo (XV.3.2) writes that Susa is shaped like a lozenge and has no fortifications.

2 See Perrot 1981 for a general description of the remains. It seems that all the buildings were planned by Darius (522–486 BC) and some of them were completed by his son Xerxes (486–65 BC).

3 An archaeomagnetic survey was used to search for any gravel foundations which might have supported an important Achaemenid building, but the results were completely negative.

4 Both the terms *tachara* and *hadish* are still to be explained, despite great efforts by the epigraphists. The Shaur palace clearly shows the simultaneous use of both terms, apparently for the same building, unless it is that each concerns a different part of it, although this hypothesis seems unlikely.

5 For the pottery from the Ville Royale, see Miroschedji 1987; for the remains of stone vessels, see Amiet 1990.

6 This point is clear from his survey despite some misdatings.

7 It should be remembered that the Susiana plain has pleasant weather only from November to March.

Achaemenid History and the Book of Daniel

by T. C. Mitchell
LONDON

The well-known engraving (Fig. 27) of the so-called Tomb of Daniel at Susa was published in 1857 in William Kennet Loftus's book, *Travels and Researches in Chaldaea and Susiana* (facing p. 322). Loftus worked at the site in 1851, but Austen Henry Layard had already visited it in 1841, and in his later book *Early Adventures*, published in 1887, he wrote about the tomb as follows: 'I found it to be a building of comparatively modern date, resembling the Imaum-Zadehs, or tombs and shrines of Musulman saints, constantly met with in Khuzistan, surmounted by a high conical dome of irregular brickwork – somewhat resembling in shape a pine-cone ... A dark inner chamber, opening upon an outer room, contained the so-called

27 Engraving showing the Tomb of Daniel at Susa.

68

tomb – a square case of plaster which might be supposed either to cover a grave or to enclose a coffin' (Layard 1887: II, 295–6). Loftus describes it in similar terms (1857: 321–3), and goes on to quote the tradition that at the time of the Islamic conquest in the seventh century AD under the Khalif 'Umar, the military commander Abu Musa Al-Asha'ri who took the area was shown a chamber at Susa sealed with a lead seal in which was a coffin containing a very large man in a shroud of gold brocade. He was said to have been an eminent man from Iraq, where he had been known as Dāniyāl Hakim, 'Daniel the Sage' (Loftus 1857: 318–19). This body was said to have been reburied subsequently in the bed of the River Karkheh, and the mosque-tomb to have been erected on the nearest bank (Le Strange 1905: 240; see also Curzon 1892: II, 311).

I refer to this tomb simply in order to eliminate it from the discussion, since it pretty clearly has nothing to do with a figure who, even if some do not accept that he lived in Neo-Babylonian or Achaemenid times, and I shall return to this question later, is named in scrolls of the first century BC from Qumran, and must therefore have been at least as early as that time.

Moreover this, the best-known 'Tomb of Daniel', is not the only one claimed, Islamic tradition indeed referring to 'Little Daniel' (*Daniyal-i asghar*) at Susa, as against 'Great Daniel' (*Daniyal-i akbar*), whose tomb was said to be at Susan, to the north of Izeh on the upper Karun (Streck 1934: 570–71; Layard 1887: I, 399–400; Le Strange 1905: 245–6), and a similar tradition states that a coffin, possibly associated with Daniel, was found at Shushtar which was reburied by order of the Khalif 'Umar (Kramers 1934: 393–5).

Sources of knowledge of the Book of Daniel

The Biblical Book of Daniel has been the subject of lively debate for generations, and it would be appropriate to outline the sources of knowledge about it and its main contents before looking at those parts which relate to the Achaemenid period. The questions connected with it are complex, and there is space here only to touch on a few points, in several instances leaving questions open.

The Book is known from a number of manuscript sources (Fig. 28) the main ones being: (a) the Massoretic text, which gives the Hebrew and Aramaic text, fixed in the early centuries of the Christian era, and passed down by the Rabbinic scholars of about the seventh to tenth centuries AD; (b) the Septuagint text, a Greek translation prepared in the last three centuries BC; (c) the Theodotionic text, the different and more literal Greek translation of the Massoretic text (or revision of the Septuagint) associated with the name of the otherwise little-known figure, Theodotion, of the second century AD, but as far as the text of Daniel is concerned, already in existence in some form by the beginning of the Christian era, and therefore sometimes known as Proto-Theodotion; (d) the Peshitta text, a Syriac translation, probably of the Massoretic text, prepared in the Syrian church during the first to third centuries AD; (e) a different and later Syriac translation by Paul, Bishop of Tella in Mesopotamia, of the Septuagint version, now mainly lost, which had been included in Origen's Hexapla (a six-column manuscript edition of the Old Testament giving the Hebrew, Greek transliteration of the Hebrew, Greek translations by Aquila and Symmachus, Septuagint, and Greek translation by Theodotion), this translation therefore being known also as the Syro-Hexapla Version; and (f) the Vulgate text, the Latin translation of the Hebrew and Aramaic text made by Eusebius Hieronymus, better known as Jerome, in the late fourth and early fifth centuries AD. Though there were a number of other versions,[2] these are the main sources which supply the text of the Book of Daniel. They differ among themselves at many points, and while the Hebrew and Aramaic of the Massoretic text provide a working basis for the student, it cannot be assumed that it represents the text precisely as originally written.

The familiar chapter and verse divisions were only introduced in the thirteenth and fourteenth centuries by Stephen Langton and Rabbi Salomon ben Ishmael respectively. The Book is traditionally divided into twelve chapters (Fig. 29), the first six consisting of narratives describing the experiences of Daniel and his friends at Babylon under various rulers from Nebuchadnezzar to Cyrus, and the last six reporting four visions experienced by Daniel under rulers from Belshazzar to Cyrus.

The two Greek versions, Septuagint and Theodotion, include additional material (Fig. 30): the story of Susanna, which precedes chapter 1; a long passage concerning the three young men and the Fiery Furnace which forms an insertion in chapter 3; and the story of Bel and the Dragon which comes at the end of chapter 12.

It is instructive, I think, to look at the dates of the surviving manuscripts of these various versions. Leaving aside the Massoretic text for the present, the main Septuagint text of Daniel was for many years known only from a manuscript of the eleventh century AD, the Codex Chisianus, now in the Vatican Library (Swete 1930: XII–XIII). In 1931, however, much of the Septuagint text of chapters 3–8 came to light on papyri of the third century AD from Egypt, now in the Chester Beatty collection in Dublin (Kenyon 1937: 17–38; 1958: 115–18). The text of Theodotion's Greek translation, however, came to replace the original Septuagint text in most manuscripts and is available for instance in the great fourth century AD manuscript, the Codex Vaticanus in Rome. For the Syriac evidence, there are Peshitta manuscripts dating from the fifth century AD onwards, and manuscripts of the Syro-Hexapla text of Paul of Tella, dating back to the seventh century AD (Roberts 1951: 226–8). Many texts of the Vulgate are known from the sixth to ninth centuries AD, a fine example being the manuscript known as the Codex Amiatinus, of the early eighth century AD, now in the Laurentinian Library in Florence (Wurthwein 1979: no. 43).

The Massoretic text presents a different picture, since for generations it was known only from medieval biblical manuscripts not earlier than the ninth to tenth centuries AD. It was this type of text on which all study was based until the discovery of the Dead Sea Scrolls in 1947. The great manuscript discoveries at Qumran in the years following 1947 brought to light a number of fragments of the text of Daniel (Barthélemy and Milik 1955: 150–52; Baillet, Milik and de Vaux 1962: 114–16; Ulrich 1987 and 1989). In these the texts, apart from some variations in spelling, agree closely with the traditional Massoretic text. The traditional Massoretic text of the Hebrew Bible is thought to have been agreed and fixed in the fifth and sixth centuries of the Christian Era, at which time other divergent manuscripts were suppressed, but for some books the existence of such divergent texts has now been demonstrated by manuscripts from Qumran which show variations from the Massoretic version. It has thus become clear that scribal alterations in transmission had led to different manuscript traditions for various books, a situation long known to the textual critic of the New Testament, but thought not to apply to the Old Testament before the Qumran discoveries. As has been mentioned, the Qumran manuscripts agree very closely with the Massoretic version of Daniel, but nevertheless there may have been a divergent Hebrew text tradition, not represented at Qumran, lying behind the Septuagint texts. In any detailed study of the Book, therefore, the other versions have to be compared. There will, however, be little occasion to do this in this short paper. The question of date must now be considered.

The linguistic setting of the Book of Daniel

I have spent some time outlining the manuscript evidence for the Book of Daniel because it is the basic material with which we have to deal, and also because I wanted to emphasise the fact that much of it is some centuries later than the date of composition of the book, whatever view is taken of that, and therefore we have to reckon with the possibility of scribal alterations in the course of transmission. It is appropriate now to look at some considerations bearing on the date of composition of the Book of Daniel. It purports to describe events during the Neo-Babylonian and Achaemenid periods, naming the rulers Nebuchadnezzar, Belshazzar, Darius the Mede (a figure who will call for further discussion), and Cyrus, that is to say the sixth and early fifth centuries BC. Many modern scholars, however, believe it to be a composition of the second century BC.

In examining the question of dating, one approach is through the languages involved. At least four come into consideration: Hebrew, Aramaic, Persian and Greek. This is because the book as we have it is partly in Hebrew and partly in Aramaic (Dan. 2:4–7:28) and contains a number of Persian and a few Greek loan-words. It also contains Babylonian loan-words (Rosenthal 1974: 57–8), but these are not significant for chronology. For this purpose, of course, only the Massoretic text is relevant, and while it may represent only one possible manuscript tradition for the Hebrew and Aramaic text, the manuscripts from Qumran give confidence that pending further evidence it is reasonable to take it as a working source. In considering at what stages of the different languages it is reasonable to place the Book of Daniel, the situation cannot be straightforward, since for none of the languages involved is there available a complete sequence of dated textual evidence against which documents can be compared.

For Hebrew there is a limited body of inscriptional evidence dating from the tenth century BC onwards, becoming sparse in the sixth century (the period of the Exile), and only becoming fuller by about the second century BC. This is actual inscriptional evidence, but for our knowledge of both the Old Testament and of Rabbinic literature we are dependent on medieval copies, in which it is necessary to reckon with the exigencies of scribal transmission.

	Date of Composition	Date of Manuscripts
Hebrew and Aramaic		
Massoretic text	?	1st cent. BC–1st cent. AD
		9th/10th century AD –
Greek		
Septuagint	3rd–1st century BC	3rd and 11th century AD
Theodotion	1st–2nd century AD	4th century AD –
Syriac		
Peshitta	1st–3rd century AD	5th century AD –
Paul of Tella	7th century AD	7th century AD –
Latin		
Vulgate	4th–5th century AD	6th century AD –

28 Manuscript sources of the Book of Daniel

The Hebrew of the Old Testament has a superficial appearance of uniformity because of the work of later scribes. However, certain features of grammar and vocabulary are generally agreed to indicate that the main body of Old Testament Literature is pre-Exilic, that is to say, pre-dates the fall of Jerusalem in 597 and 586 BC, but it is also generally agreed that certain books, notably Ezra, Nehemiah, Chronicles, Esther and Daniel, are late. In these terms, the Hebrew of the Book of Daniel is late, but the question is, how late? Recent studies, notably of the Book of Ezekiel (Rooker 1990), suggest that, while the Hebrew of Daniel is clearly late, there is no need to assume a date later than about the fifth century, the date normally assigned to Ezra and Nehemiah. In other words a date in the Achaemenid period is quite plausible. It might be argued, of course, that early features in the Book of Daniel could be the result of archaising, so this case should not be overstated, but when this evidence is set beside that from Aramaic and Iranian, a fifth- or even late sixth-century date remains a plausible possibility.

The situation concerning Aramaic is more complex in view of the much wider range of evidence, arising from the widespread use of Aramaic in the Near East from the first half of the first millennium BC onwards, and its use as the lingua franca of the Achaemenid Empire. A considerable number of inscriptions are known. Various chronological schemes have been proposed, a reasonable one being that of Joseph Fitzmyer according to which Old Aramaic runs from the earliest inscriptions until about 700 BC, Official Aramaic, otherwise known as Imperial Aramaic, until 300 or 200 BC, Middle Aramaic until AD 200, and finally Late Aramaic up to the coming of Islam (Fitzmyer 1979: 57–84). On present evidence the Aramaic of Daniel, which may be classified as Official Aramaic, is not inconsistent with a date in the Achaemenid period, that is to say in the fifth or fourth, and quite plausibly the late sixth, century BC (see Kitchen 1965). It is interesting to note that Professor Fitzmyer, whose chronological subdivisions have been adopted here, originally set the end of Official Aramaic at *c*.300 BC, but lowered it to *c*.200 BC partly on the basis of what he calls 'the problem of the Aramaic of Daniel', but he says 'even that should not be pressed too rigidly' (Fitzmyer 1979: 77 n.32).

1	Daniel's Training in Babylon	7	Daniel's Dream of Four Beasts [Aramaic]
2	Nebuchadnezzar's Dream of a Statue [partly Aramaic]	8	Daniel's Vision of a Ram and Goat
3	The Image of Gold and the Fiery Furnace [Aramaic]	9	Daniel's Vision of Seventy Weeks
4	Nebuchadnezzar's Dream of a Tree [Aramaic]	10	Daniel's Vision of the Future: Preparation
5	Belshazzar's Feast [Aramaic]	11	Daniel's Vision of the Future: World History
6	Daniel in the Lions' Den [Aramaic]	12	Daniel's Vision of the Future: The End Times

29 Contents of the Massoretic version of the Book of Daniel

	Susanna		
1	Daniel's Training in Babylon	7	Daniel's Dream of Four Beasts
2	Nebuchadnezzar's Dream of a Statue	8	Daniel's Vision of a Ram and Goat
3	The Image of Gold and the Fiery Furnace	9	Daniel's Vision of Seventy Weeks
	[Prayer of the Three Israelites] (24–90)	10	Daniel's Vision of the Future: Preparation
	The Fiery Furnace (91–7)	11	Daniel's Vision of the Future: World History
4	Nebuchadnezzar's Dream of a Tree	12	Daniel's Vision of the Future: The End Times
5	Belshazzar's Feast		Bel and the Dragon
6	Daniel in the Lions' Den		

30 Contents of the Greek versions of the Book of Daniel

The fact is that the later dating is based to a large extent on other than linguistic grounds.[3]

There are considerable numbers of Iranian loan-words in the Aramaic part of the Book of Daniel, and a smaller number in the Hebrew passages. Some of these are found also in Ezra and Esther, and more sparsely in Chronicles and Ecclesiastes (Qoheleth). There are also substantial numbers of Iranian loan-words in Babylonian texts and Aramaic inscriptions of the fifth and fourth centuries BC, and against this background, and other evidence that words not attested until later were nevertheless probably borrowed in Achaemenid times (Shaked 1987: 259), the Aramaic of the Book of Daniel can be seen to fit plausibly in this period. On this basis a sixth or fifth century BC date is possible.

It is generally agreed that there are three Greek loan-words in the Book of Daniel. These all appear to be the names of musical instruments, *qaytĕrōs* from *kitharis*, 'lyre', *pĕsantĕrîn* from *psalterion*, possibly another kind of lyre, and *sûmpōnĕyâ*, probably from some form like *sumphōnia*, or *tumpanon*, perhaps referring to a type of tambour. We have argued elsewhere that musical instruments with Greek names are quite possible in sixth or fifth century BC Babylonia (Mitchell and Joyce 1965), and their presence should be seen against the background of a considerable Greek presence in the Near East by the sixth century BC (Mitchell 1992: 136).

On the basis of the languages and loan-words in Daniel, therefore, it seems to me reasonable to see it as a composition largely of the fifth century BC, that is to say roughly the first century of the Achaemenid Empire, making use of earlier material from the sixth century BC. This could account for one of the peculiarities of the Book which is the use of the Persian word *'aḥašdarpan*, 'satrap', to refer to officers under Nebuchadnezzar, rather perhaps in the way we would speak of Alexander the Great as a 'general' (rather than a *strategos* or a *basileus*).

Other indications of date

This is not to say that the Book of Daniel in its present form has not suffered from errors in scribal transmission, and many questions concerning it are likely to remain unresolved. As has been mentioned, the most common view of the date of the Book of Daniel is that it was composed in the second century, around 165 BC, in the period of persecution under Antiochus IV Epiphanes (175–164 BC) (Fohrer 1970: 477–8). This conclusion depends largely on the apparent precision with which visions described in the second half of the book match actual events, leading up to the prophecy in 11:31, concerning the 'King of the North', presumed to be one of the Seleucids, that 'His armed forces will rise up to desecrate the temple fortress and will abolish the daily sacrifice. Then they will set up the abomination of desolation' (*haššiqqûṣ mešômēm*, 'the abominable (thing) that makes desolate' or 'the abomination from desolation'; found also in slightly different wording in 9:27 and 12:11), which is taken to refer to the desecration of the Temple in Jerusalem by Antiochus in about 167 BC (Goldstein 1976: 163, 224–5). The book does not, however, mention the death of Antiochus, which took place in 164 BC, so it is concluded that it was completed between 167 and 164 BC.

In general, the alleged precision of the match between the visionary language in Daniel and events culminating in about 167 BC is said to be an example of a type of prophecy known from Roman documents of the Hellenistic period, in which the device known as *vaticinium ex eventu*, 'a prophecy from an outcome', that is to say description of a past event as if it were in the future, is employed (Fohrer 1970: 476–7). This type of composition is also known, however, in various forms in Akkadian texts (see Grayson 1989–90), including one example, sometimes known as the 'Uruk prophecy', which, though the actual surviving tablet probably dates from the early Achaemenid period, may have been composed in the earlier part of the sixth century BC, so similarity of literary genre does not necessarily indicate a Hellenistic date.

There are many matters for which there is not sufficient space for discussion here, such as the fact that in the Massoretic Bible the Book of Daniel is not placed with the Prophets (see, for example, Young 1949: 20–21).[4] I will now turn, however, to the information it gives about rulers and places relevant to the Persian period. A considerable part of the Book is set in the

Neo-Babylonian period, but it also carries the story over into the time of the Achaemenid Empire.

The Achaemenid period in the Book of Daniel

Two Iranian rulers are mentioned. 'Cyrus the king' (*kôreš hammelek*) is named in a statement that Daniel continued to his first year (Dan 1:21), and he is referred to as 'Cyrus the Persian' (*kôreš parsāyā'*) in a statement that Daniel prospered in his reign (6:29). Finally one of Daniel's visions is dated to the third year of 'Cyrus king of Persia' (*kôreš melek pāras*) (10:1). There is no difficulty in seeing this as Cyrus II, the Great, the conqueror of Babylon in 539 BC. The statements about him in Daniel, though they do not add to what is known from other sources, do not raise any problems.

The same cannot be said for the other Iranian ruler mentioned in Daniel. This is the figure referred to as 'Darius the Mede' (*dārĕyāweš mādāyā'*), who is said to have 'received the kingdom' (*qabbēl malkûtā'*) from Belshazzar after the latter's death and the fall of the Neo-Babylonian empire (5:30). The word 'received' in relation to the kingdom could be interpreted in various ways, including that he was simply made governor. This is supported by another passage where he is said to have been *hāmlak*, 'made king' or 'made ruler' (9:1), where the passive of the verb 'to rule, be king' is used. Further information about him is that: (a) he was the 'son of *'ăḥašwērôš*' (9:1), a name also found in the book of Esther (10:1) where it is normally taken to refer to 'Xerxes'; (b) he was 'of the seed of the Medes' (*mizzera' mādāy*) (9:1); (c) he was 62 years old when he came to power (5: 30); and (d) he set 120 satraps (*'ăḥašdarpĕnayyā'*) over the kingdom (6:1).

No 'Darius the Mede' is known from the ancient sources, and there has been much speculation about his identity. Perhaps the simplest suggestion is that he is a fictitious figure invented by a writer in the Hellenistic period who had no reliable knowledge of the early Achaemenid period, the result of 'a conflation of confused traditions', as H.H. Rowley put it many years ago (Rowley 1935: 54). A variation of this view, held by many today, is that 'Darius the Mede' was actually Darius I (521–486 BC) misplaced chronologically (Hartman and Di Lella 1978: 36), such discrepancies with the Daniel account as that he was not an immediate successor to the Neo-Babylonian dynasty, and that he was a Persian rather than a Mede, being set down to the unreliability of the author.

Others would identify Darius the Mede as Cyrus II (the Great) (e.g. Hinz 1970: col. 1026). It is relevant to mention here that according to the Hellenistic Greek author Dinon (or Deinon) of Colophon, perhaps *c.* 300 BC, Cyrus II was forty years old when he became king, and reigned for thirty years (Jacoby 1958: 525–6, no. 10; quoted by Cicero, *De Divinatione* I.46). In this case, since he died in 530 BC, he would have been born in about 600 BC and would therefore have been about sixty at the time of the conquest of Babylon in 539 BC. Although Dinon is not regarded as a reliable authority (see e.g. Smith 1944: 29), one recent assessment, while concluding that he did invent some of his data, rates him as 'a reasonably serious and careful historian' (Stevenson 1987: 35). This identification could find support in another suggestion arising from the phrase concerning Daniel (6:28) which appears in most translations as 'he prospered in the reign of Darius and in the reign of Cyrus the Persian'. It has been pointed out that the conjunction wĕ, here translated 'and', can also mean 'that is to say, namely', as for example in 1 Chronicles 5:26 (Wiseman 1965: 12–13). On this basis the phrase might be translated 'he prospered in the reign of Darius, that is to say in the reign of Cyrus the Persian', Darius the Mede in that case being simply another title of Cyrus. Though Cyrus is described in his inscriptions as an Achaemenid, and in Daniel as 'the Persian', the fact that he was the grandson, through his mother, of Astyages the Mede, might be taken to justify his being described as 'of the seed of the Medes'. The name Darius means something like 'He who holds fast to the good' (Brandenstein and Mayrhofer 1964: 115; Kent 1950: 189), so one possibility is that at one stage it was a title.

Another suggestion which deserves consideration is that 'Darius the Mede' was Gubaru, the governor of Gutium, who took Babylon on behalf of Cyrus, and who, according to the Nabonidus Chronicle, ruled there briefly, appointing governors (paḥati), before his early death (Grayson 1975: 109–10). This man is surely to be identified with the Gobryas described in the Cyropaedia of Xenophon as an elderly man at the time of Cyrus' Babylonian campaign (4:6:1). He has to be distinguished from another senior officer of Cyrus, also named Gubaru, who was governor of the large area of Babylon and Syria from at least 535 to 525 BC, and also from a third Gobryas, a follower of Darius I, who is mentioned by Herodotus (Mitchell 1991: 434). As to the ethnic affiliations of the first Gubaru, geographically speaking the area known in the third and second millennia BC as 'Gutium' was the 'Media' of the first millennium BC. To describe Gubaru as governor of Gutium therefore is in effect to name him governor of Media, and to open up the possibility that he was actually of Median birth himself.[5] This is perhaps rather a long shot, but if it were correct, the use of the Akkadian word paḥatu in the Nabonidus Chronicle for the governors appointed by Gubaru, would be in tune with the use of the Persian word hšathrapavam, Biblical 'aḥašdarpan, in Daniel for the appointees of Darius the Mede. A further argument adduced in favour of this identification is based on the observation that in the date formulae of cuneiform economic texts at the beginning of the reign of Cyrus there is an interruption of fourteen months in the usual pattern carried over from the Neo-Babylonian period. This standard pattern gives the month, day and year followed, for example, by 'Nabonidus king of Babylon', usually expanded in the Achaemenid period to, for example, 'Cyrus king of Babylon, king of Countries'. During the final four months of Cyrus' accession year (following his conquest of Babylon) and the first ten months of his first year (October 539 to December 538 BC) this is replaced by the shortened formula 'Cyrus king of Countries', but after this period the pattern 'Cyrus king of Babylon, king of Countries' is resumed. This implies that during the fourteen months another person served as 'King of Babylon', being in this sense co-regent with Cyrus, and it is argued that this could have been Gubaru (Shea 1971–72; 1982). Against this it has been pointed out that there are two texts from this period dated by the formula 'month X, day X, year 1, Cyrus king of Countries, Cambyses king of Babylon', the ruler of Babylon during at least part of this fourteen months therefore having been Cambyses (Grabbe 1988: 199–294), the son and ultimate successor of Cyrus. However, these two texts date from the months April/May and May/June respectively of 538 BC, and therefore do not exclude another and different co-regent, not necessarily Gubaru, from having been ruler of Babylon during the period between October 539 and April 538 BC. Against this being Gubaru is the fact that the Babylonian Chronicle states that Ugbaru (probably a variant form of Gubaru) died on 6 November 539 BC (Grayson 1975: 110), very shortly after Cyrus entered Babylon (on 29 October 539). On the other hand, if Gubaru and Ugbaru were distinct individuals this objection would not apply. It has also been argued that his death might actually have been in the following year (18 October 538). These are tenuous considerations, however, and can only be ranked as further possibilities. The question of the identity of Darius the Mede, therefore, including the possibility that a third individual, neither Cyrus nor Gubaru, was king of Babylon during the first few months of Cyrus' reign, must remain open.[6]

Another figure who needs to be considered is the officer who is referred to as the *rab sârîs*, 'chief officer', of Nebuchadnezzar, whose name is given as Ashpenaz (1:3). This seems to be an Iranian name, which would be unusual in the sixth century BC. It is unknown in any ancient source, but if it is compounded from the element *asp-*, 'horse', this could point to a Median origin, since the Old Persian form was *asa* as against *aspa* in Median and Avestan (Bartholomae 1904: 215–16; Brandenstein and Mayrhofer 1964: 106; Kent 1950: 173).[7] There are, of course, many references to Media in the Assyrian inscriptions, dating from as early as the ninth century BC onwards, so a Median at the court of Nebuchadnezzar would not be improbable.

Finally, an interesting reference at the beginning of chapter 8, dated to the 3rd year of Belshazzar, which would have been about 550 BC, states that Daniel had a vision in which he saw himself 'at the citadel of Susa (*běšûšan habîrâ*), which is in the province of Elam (*bě'ēlām hammědînâ*), and ... by the Ulai canal (*'ûbāl 'ûlāy*)'. The word here translated 'canal' is *'ûbāl*, which, as Waterman suggested long ago (1947) has the general sense of carrying water, something perhaps more appropriate to a man-made canal than to a main stream. If this is so, it might be taken into account in the question of identification of the Ulai known from the cuneiform inscriptions. There is no agreement about this, there being advocates of the Karun, the Karkheh, or, perhaps favoured by the text of Daniel, one of the canals between the two such as the Shaur. Another clue might be the location of the city of Madaktu, shown on the bank of the Ulai in the well-known dramatic series of Assyrian reliefs illustrating Ashurbanipal's defeat of the Elamites, but there is no general agreement about the location of this city. Nothing further can be gleaned from the account in Daniel.

There is thus only a limited amount of information about the Achaemenid period to be derived from the Book of Daniel, but as I have suggested earlier, I think there are good arguments for seeing the book, substantially in its present form, more as a product of the Achaemenid period, perhaps the fifth century BC, than of the Hellenistic period, the second century BC. There was no doubt scribal activity over the generations, beginning with the late sixth century, and the text as we have it is probably not what it was in the fifth century, but in view of the considerable limitations to our knowledge which I have sought to outline earlier I think it is sensible to treat it with respect, and continue to study it with an open mind.

Notes

1   Also reproduced in Driver 1900: frontispiece. For other early views of the tomb see Ghirshman 1970: opp 192, and Dieulafoy 1888: p.81.

2   It is appropriate in the context of this symposium to mention also a fragmentary Sogdian text from Bulayik in Turfan, which includes references to three episodes concerning Daniel: his training in Babylon; Nebuchadnezzar's dream of a statue; and Bel and the Dragon (Sims-Williams 1993). All of these episodes were probably taken from Paul of Tella's Syriac translation of the Septuagint.

3   For a polemical discussion of this aspect, which is far from new, see for example Pusey 1892: 4–8, 234–40.

4   Other such matters will be discussed in my commentary on Daniel, in preparation.

5   On Gutians and Medes, see Burstein 1978: 33–5; Xenophon quotes Gubaru as saying that he was an Assyrian by birth (Cyropaedia IV.6:2), but this testimony is weakened by the fact that in this passage Assyrian means Babylonian.

6   For a spirited restatement of the view that Darius the Mede was a fictitious character, see Grabbe 1988.

7   Justi however (1895: 46), suggests a connection with Pahlawi *aspanj*, 'guest; ease, repose'; cf. Mackenzie 1971: 12, *aspinj*, 'hospitality, inn'.

Bibliography

Aaboe, A., *et al.*, 1991. 'Saros cycle dates and related Babylonian astronomical texts', *Transactions of the American Philosophical Society* 81/6: 1–75.

Alizadeh, A., 1985. 'A tomb of the Neo-Elamite period at Arjan, near Behbahan', *Archaeologische Mitteilungen aus Iran* 18: 49–73.

Amiet, P., 1972. 'Les ivoires achéménides de Suse', *Syria* 49: 167–91, 319–37.

Amiet, P., 1974. 'Quelques observations sur le palais de Darius à Suse', *Syria* 51: 65–73.

Amiet, P., 1988. *Suse: 6000 ans d'histoire*, Paris.

Amiet, P., 1990. 'Quelques épaves de la vaisselle royale perse de Suse', in Vallat, F. (ed.), *Contribution à l'histoire de l'Iran: Mélanges offerts à Jean Perrot*, Paris: 213–24.

Baillet, M., Milik, J.T., and de Vaux, R., 1962. *Les 'petites grottes' de Qumran*, Discoveries in the Judaean Desert III, Oxford.

Baird, D., Campbell, S., and Watkins, T. (eds), 1995. *Excavations at Kharabeh Shattani* II, University of Edinburgh, Department of Archaeology, Occasional Paper no. 18, Edinburgh.

Barag, D., 1968. 'An unpublished Achaemenid cut glass bowl from Nippur', *Journal of Glass Studies* X: 17–20.

Barag, D., 1985. *Catalogue of Western Asiatic Glass in the British Museum* I, London.

Barnett, R.D., 1969. 'Anath, Ba'al and Pasargadae', *Mélanges de l' Université Saint-Joseph* 45: 407–22.

Barthélemy, D., and Milik, J.T., 1955. *Qumran Cave I*, Discoveries in the Judaean Desert I, Oxford.

Bartholomae, C., 1904. *Altiranisches Wörterbuch*, Berlin.

Bissing, Fr. W. von, 1942. 'Ägyptische und ägyptisierende Alabastergefässe aus den deutschen Ausgrabungen in Babylon', *Zeitschrift für Assyriologie* 47: 26–49.

Black, J. and Green, A., 1992. *Gods, Demons and Symbols of Ancient Mesopotamia*, London.

Boehmer, R. M., 1973. 'Forschungen in und um Mudjesir', *Archäologischer Anzeiger*: 479–521.

Bollweg, J., 1988. 'Protoachämenidische Siegelbilder', *Archäologische Mitteilungen aus Iran* 21: 53–61.

Boucharlat, R., and Labrousse, A., 1979. 'Le palais d'Artaxerxès II sur la rive droite du Chaour à Suse', *Cahiers de la Délégation Archéologique Française en Iran* 10: 21–136.

Boucharlat, R., 1985. 'Suse, marché agricole ou relais du grand commerce. Suse et la Susiane à l'époque des grands empires', *Paléorient* 11/2: 71–81.

Boucharlat, R., and Shahidi, H., 1987. 'Fragments architecturaux de type achéménide. Découvertes fortuites dans la ville de Shoush 1976-1979', *Cahiers de la Délégation Archéologique Française en Iran* 15: 313–27.

Boucharlat, R., 1990a. 'Suse et la Susiane à l'époque achéménide. Données archéologiques', *Achaemenid History* IV: 149–75.

Boucharlat, R., 1990b. 'La fin des palais

achéménides de Suse: une mort naturelle', in Vallat, F. (ed.), *Contribution à l'histoire de l'Iran: Mélanges offerts à Jean Perrot*, Paris: 225–33.

Brandenstein, W., and Mayrhofer, M., 1964. *Handbuch des Altpersischen*, Wiesbaden.

Brentjes, B., 1995. 'The history of Elam and Achaemenid Persia: an overview', in Sasson, J.M. (ed.), *Civilizations of the Ancient Near East* II, New York: 1001–21.

Briant, P., 1988. 'Le nomadisme du Grand Roi', *Iranica Antiqua* 23: 253–73.

Burstein, S.M., 1978. *The Babyloniaca of Berossus*, Sources from the Ancient Near East I/5, Malibu.

Calmeyer, P., 1994. 'Babylonische und assyrische Elemente in der achaimenidischen Kunst', *Achaemenid History* VIII: 131–47.

Cameron, G. G., 1936. *History of Early Iran*, Chicago.

Cameron, G.G., 1941. 'Darius and Xerxes in Babylonia', *The American Journal of Semitic Languages and Literatures* LVIII: 314–25.

Cameron, G.G., 1948. *Persepolis Treasury Tablets*, Oriental Institute Publications 65, Chicago.

Cameron, G.G., 1965. 'New tablets from the Persepolis treasury', *Journal of Near Eastern Studies* 24:167–92.

Cardascia, G., 1951. *Les archives des Murašû*, Paris.

Cardascia, G., 1989. 'Babylon under the Achaemenids', *Encyclopaedia Iranica* III: 325–6.

Carter, E., 1994. 'Bridging the gap between the Elamites and the Persians in south-eastern Khuzistan', *Achaemenid History* VIII: 65–95.

Curtis, J.E., 1983. 'Some axe-heads from Chagar Bazar and Nimrud', *Iraq* XLV: 73–81.

Curtis, J.E., 1989. *Excavations at Qasrij Cliff and Khirbet Qasrij*, London.

Curtis, J.E., 1993. 'William Kennett Loftus and his excavations at Susa', *Iranica Antiqua* 28: 1–55.

Curtis, J.E. (ed.), 1995. *Later Mesopotamia and Iran: Tribes and Empires 1600–539 BC*, Proceedings of a Seminar in Memory of Vladimir G. Lukonin, London.

Curtis, J.E., and Reade, J.E. (eds) 1995. *Art and Empire: Treasures from Assyria in the British Museum*, London.

Curtis, J.E., Cowell, M.R., and Walker, C.B.F., 1995. 'A silver bowl of Artaxerxes I', *Iran* XXXIII: 149–53.

Curzon, G.N., 1892. *Persia and the Persian Question*, 2 vols., London.

Dalley, S., 1993. 'Nineveh after 612 BC', *Altorientalische Forschungen* 20: 134–47.

Dalton, O.M., 1964. *The Treasure of the Oxus with Other Examples of Early Oriental Metal-Work*, 3rd edition, London.

Dandamayev, M., 1969. 'Achaemenid Babylonia', in Diakonoff, I.M. (ed.), *Ancient Mesopotamia*, Moscow: 296–310.

Dandamayev, M., 1987. 'Achaemenid Athurā', *Encyclopaedia Iranica* II: 816.

Dandamayev, M., 1989. 'History of Babylonia in the Median and Achaemenid Periods', *Encyclopaedia Iranica* III: 326–34.

Dandamayev, M., 1993. 'Xerxes and the Esagila Temple in Babylon', *Bulletin of the Asia Institute*, new series 7: 41–5.

Dayton, J. 1978. *Minerals, Metals, Glazing and Man*, London.

Dieulafoy, J., 1888. *À Suse: Journal des fouilles 1884–1886*, Paris.

Dieulafoy, M., 1893. *L'acropole de Suse, d'après les fouilles exécutées en 1884, 1885, 1886*, Paris.

Driver, S.R., 1900. *Daniel*, Cambridge Bible for Schools and Colleges, Cambridge.

Dubberstein, W.H., 1939. 'Comparative prices in later Babylonia (625–400 BC)', *The American Journal of Semitic Languages and Literatures* LVI: 20-43.

Edmonds, C.J., 1934. 'A Tomb in Kurdistan', *Iraq* 1: 183–92.

Elayi, J., and Elayi, A.G., 1992. 'Nouvelle datation d'une tombe achéménide de Suse', *Studia Iranica* 21: 265–70.

Fitzmyer, J.A., 1979. *A Wandering Aramaean: Collected Aramaic Essays*, Missoula.

Fleming, D., 1989. 'Eggshell ware pottery in Achaemenid Mesopotamia', *Iraq* 51: 65–185.

Fohrer, G., 1970. *Introduction to the Old Testament*, London.

Frame, G., 1992. *Babylonia 689–627 BC: A Political History*, Istanbul.

Francfort, H.-P., 1977. 'Le plan des maisons gréco-bactriennes et le problème des structures de "type megaron" en Asie Centrale et en Iran', in Deshayes, J. (ed.), *Le Plateau Iranien et l'Asie Centrale*, Paris: 267–80.

Frye, R., 1962. *The Heritage of Persia*, London.

Gall, H., von, 1988. 'Das Felsgrab von Qizqapan. Ein Denkmal aus dem Umfeld der Achämenidischen Königsstrasse', *Baghdader Mitteilungen* 19: 557–82.

Garrison, M.B., 1991. 'Seals and the elite at Persepolis: some observations on early Achaemenid Persian art', *Ars Orientalis* 21: 1–29.

Garrison, M.B., and Root, M.C., forthcoming. *Seal Impressions on the Persepolis Fortification Tablets, with notes on the inscriptions by C.E. Jones*, Fascicule II, Oriental Institute Publications, Chicago.

Gasche, H., 1991. 'Héritages susiens dans l'architecture achéménide en Babylonie (sommaire)', *Orient Express* 1: 20–21.

Gasche, H., 1995. 'Autour des Dix-Mille: vestiges archéologiques dans les environs du "Mur de Médie", in Briant, P. (ed.), *Dans les pas des Dix-Mille*, PALLAS 43, Toulouse: 173–99.

Ghirshman, R., 1954. *Village perse-achéménide*, Mémoires de la Mission Archéologique en Iran 36, Paris.

Ghirshman, R., 1965. 'Suse au temps des Sukkalmah', *Arts Asiatiques* XI: 3–21.

Ghirshman, R., 1966. *Tchoga Zanbil* I: *La Ziggurat*, Mémoires de la Délégation Archéologique en Iran 39, Paris.

Ghirshman, T., 1970. *Archéologie malgré moi*, Paris.

Ghirshman, R., 1976. *Terrasses sacrées de Bard-è Néchandeh et Masjid-i Solaiman*, Mémoires de la Délégation Archéologique en Iran 44, Paris.

Goldstein, J.A., 1976. *I Maccabees*, Anchor Bible 41, New York.

Goodwin, J., 1995. 'The first millennium BC pottery', in Baird, D., *et al.* (eds) 1995: 91–141.

Grabbe, L.L., 1988. 'Another Look at the *Gestalt* of "Darius the Mede"', *Catholic Biblical Quarterly* 50: 198–213.

Grayson, A.K., 1975. *Assyrian and Babylonian Chronicles*, Texts from Cuneiform Sources 5, Locust Valley, New York.

Grayson, A.K., 1989–90. 'The Babylonian origin of apocalyptic literature', *Atti del'Istituto Veneto di Scienze, Lettere ed Arti* 148:203–18.

Grayson, A.K., 1996. *Assyrian Rulers of the Early First Millennium BC, II (858–745 BC)*, RIMA 3, Toronto.

Green, A., 1994. 'Mischwesen', *Reallexikon der Assyriologie* 8: 246–64.

Gropp, G., 1979. 'Zwei achämenidische Gefässe mit Inschriften', *Archäologische Mitteilungen aus Iran* 12: 321–8.

Guillini, G., *et al.* (eds), 1985. *The Land between Two Rivers*, exhibition catalogue, Turin.

Haerinck, E., 1973. 'Le palais achéménide de Babylone', *Iranica Antiqua* X: 108–32.

Haerinck, E., 1987. 'La neuvième satrapie: archéologie confronte histoire?', *Achaemenid History* I: 139–45.

Haerinck, E., 1990a. 'La Mésopotamie sous les Achéménides: un bilan', in Gnoli, G., and Panaino, A. (eds) *Proceedings of the First European Conference of Iranian Studies. Part 1. Old and Middle Iranian Studies*, Rome: 159–65.

Haerinck, E., 1990b. 'Babylon unter der Herrschaft der Achaemeniden', in Koldewey, R., *Das wieder erstehende Babylon*, new edition by B. Hrouda, Munich: 372–84.

Haller, A., 1954. *Die Gräber und Grüfte von Assur*, WVDO-G 65, Berlin.

Hallock, R.T., 1960. 'A new look at the Persepolis Treasury Tablets', *Journal of Near Eastern Studies* 19: 90–100.

Hallock, R.T., 1969. *Persepolis Fortification Tablets*, Oriental Institute Publications 92, Chicago.

Hallock, R. T., 1977. 'The use of seals on the Perspolis Fortification Tablets', *Seals and Sealing in the Ancient Near East*, Bibliotheca Mesopotamica 6: 127–33.

Hansman, J., 1972. 'Elamites, Achaemenians and Anshan', *Iran* 10: 101–24.

Harper, P.O., Aruz, J., and Tallon, F. (eds), 1992. *The Royal City of Susa: Ancient Near Eastern Treasures in the Louvre*, New York.

Hartman, L.F., and Di Lella, A.A., 1978. *The Book of Daniel*, Anchor Bible 23, New York.

Hinz, W., 1970. 'Persis', *Paulys Realencyclopädie der klassischen Altertumswissenshaft* Supplementband XII: cols. 1022–38

Hrouda, B., 1962. *Tell Halaf 4: Die Kleinfunde aus historischer Zeit*, Berlin.

Huber, P.J., 1973. *Babylonian Eclipse Observations 750 BC to 0*, privately circulated typescript.

Jacoby, F., 1958. *Die Fragmente der Griechischen Historiker* III/C/1, Leiden.

Joannès, F., 1994. 'Métaux précieux et moyens de paiement en Babylonie achéménide et hellénistique', *Transeuphratène* 8: 137–44.

Joannès, F., 1995, 'L'itinéraire des Dix-Mille en Mésopotamie et l' apport des sources cunéiformes', in Briant, P. (ed.), *Dans le pas de Dix-Mille*, PALLAS 43, Toulouse: 173–99.

Justi, F., 1895. *Iranisches Namenbuch*, Marburg.

Kambakhsh Fard, S., 1995. 'The rock inscription and the rock relief at Bisitun', in Kambakhsh Fard, S., *The Anahita Temple at Kangavar*, Iranian Cultural Heritage Organization 23, Tehran: 372–98 (in Persian).

Kawami, T., 1972. 'A possible source for the scuptures of the Audience Hall, Pasargadae', *Iran* X: 146–48.

Kent, R.G., 1953. *Old Persian: Grammar, Texts, Lexicon*, New Haven, Connecticut.

Kenyon, F.G., 1937. *The Chester Beatty Biblical Papyri* VII, London.

Kervran, M., *et al.*, 1972. 'Une statue de Darius découverte à Suse', *Journal Asiatique* 260: 235–66.

Kitchen, K.A., 1965. 'The Aramaic of Daniel', in Wiseman, D.J., *et al.*, *Notes on Some Problems in the Book of Daniel*, London: 31–79.

Klengel, H., 1962. 'Babylon zur Zeit der Perser, Griechen und Parther', *Forschungen und Berichte* 5: 40–53.

Koldewey, R., 1914. *The Excavations at Babylon*, London.

Koldewey, R., 1931. *Die Königsburgen von Babylon*,

WVDO-G 55, Leipzig.

Kramers, J.H., 1934. 'Shuster', *The Encyclopaedia of Islam* IV: 393–5.

Kugler, F.X., 1909–24. *Sternkunde und Sterndienst in Babel* II, Munster.

Kuhrt, A., and Sherwin-White, S.M., 1987. 'Xerxes' destruction of Babylonian temples', *Achaemenid History* II: 69–78.

Kuhrt, A., 1988. 'Babylonia from Cyrus to Xerxes', *Cambridge Ancient History* IV, second edition: 112–38.

Kuhrt, A., 1995. 'The Assyrian heartland in the Achaemenid period', in Briant, P. (ed.), *Dans les pas des Dix-Mille*, PALLAS 43, Toulouse: 239–54.

Labrousse, A., and Boucharlat, R., 1972. 'La fouille du palais du Chaour à Suse en 1970 et 1970', *Cahiers de la Délégation Archéologique Française en Iran* 2: 61–167.

Layard, A.H., 1853. *Discoveries in the Ruins of Nineveh and Babylon*, London.

Layard, A.H., 1887. *Early Adventures in Persia, Susiana, and Babylonia*, 2 vols., London.

Le Strange, G., 1905. *The Lands of the Eastern Caliphate*, Cambridge.

Legrain, L., 1925. *Culture of the Babylonians*, Publications of the Babylonian Section, University of Pennsylvania XIV, Philadelphia.

Liagre Böhl, F.M. de, 1962. 'Die babylonischen Prätendenten zur Zeit des Xerxes', *Bibliotheca Orientalis* 19: 110–14.

Loftus, W.K., 1857. *Travels and Researches in Chaldaea and Susiana*, London.

Loud, G., and Altman, C.B., 1938. *Khorsabad* II: *The Citadel and the Town*, Oriental Institute Publications 40, Chicago.

Luschey, H., 1939. *Die Phiale*, Bleicherode am Harz.

Luschey, H., 1983. 'Die Darius-Statuen aus Susa und ihre Rekonstruktion', in Koch, H., and Mackenzie, D.M. (eds), *Kunst, Kultur und Geschichte der Achämenidenzeit und ihr Fortleben*, AMI Ergänzungsband 10: 191–206.

Mackenzie, D.N., 1971. *A Concise Pahlavi Dictionary*, London.

Mallowan, M.E.L., 1966. *Nimrud and its Remains*, 2 vols, London.

Metzler, D., 1975. 'Wandteppiche mit Bildern der Perserkriege im Achämenidenpalast zu Babylon', *Mitteilungen der Deutschen Archäologen – Verbandes* 6: 37–8.

Meuleau, M., 1965. 'Mesopotamien in der Perserzeit', *Fischer Weltgeschichte* 5, Frankfurt am Main: 330–55.

Miroschedji, P. de, 1985. 'La fin du royaume d'Anšan et de Suse et la naissance de l'empire perse', *Zeitschrift für Assyriologie* 75: 266–306.

Miroschedji, P. de, 1987. 'Fouilles du chantier Ville Royale II à Suse (1975–1977). II. Niveaux d'époques achéménide, séleucide, parthe et islamique', *Cahiers de la Délégation Archéologique Française en Iran* 15: 11–143.

Mitchell, T.C., and Joyce, R., 1965. 'The musical instruments in Nebuchadnezzar's orchestra', in Wiseman, D.J., et al., *Notes on Some Problems in the Book of Daniel*, London: 19–27.

Mitchell, T.C., 1991. 'The Babylonian exile and the restoration of the Jews in Palestine (586–c.500 BC)', *Cambridge Ancient History* III/2 (second edition), Cambridge: 410–60

Mitchell, T.C., 1992. 'The Music of the Old Testament Reconsidered', *Palestine Exploration Quarterly* 124: 124–43.

Moorey, P.R.S., 1980a. *Cemeteries of the First Millennium BC at Deve Hüyük*, BAR–S87, Oxford.

Moorey, P.R.S., 1980b. 'Metal wine-sets in the Ancient Near East', *Iranica Antiqua* XV: 181–97.

Moorey, P.R.S., 1994. *Ancient Mesopotamian Materials and Industries: the Archaeological Evidence*, Oxford.

Morgan, J., de, 1905. 'Découverte d'une sépulture achéménide à Suse', *Mémoires de la Délégation en Perse* VIII: 29–58.

Mousavi, A., 1994. 'Une brique à decor polychrome de l'Iran occidental (VIIIe-VIIe s. av. J.-C.), *Studia Iranica* 23: 7–18.

Muscarella, O.W., 1995. 'Art and Archaeology of Western Iran in Prehistory', in Sasson, J.M. (ed.), *Civilizations of the Ancient Near East* II, New York: 981–99.

Neugebauer, O., 1975. *History of Ancient Mathematical Astronomy*, New York.

Neugebauer, O., 1988. 'A Babylonian lunar ephemeris from Roman Egypt', in Leichty, E., et al. (eds), *A Scientific Humanist: Studies in Memory of Abraham Sachs*, Philadelphia: 301–4.

Nylander, C., 1979. 'Achaemenid Imperial Art', in Larsen, M.T. (ed.), *Power and Propaganda: a Symposium on Ancient Empires*, Mesopotamia 7, Copenhagen: 345–59.

Oates, D., and J., 1958. 'Nimrud 1957: the Hellenistic settlement', *Iraq* XX: 114–57.

Otto, H., 1944. 'Ein achämenidischer Goldwidder', *Zeitschrift für Assyriologie* 48: 9–22.

Parker, R.A., and Dubberstein, W.H., 1956. *Babylonian Chronology 626 BC–AD 75*, Providence, Rhode Island.

Parrot, A., 1961. *Nineveh and Babylon*, London.

Perrot, J., 1981 'L'architecture militaire et palatiale des Achéménides à Suse', in *150 Jahre Deutsches Archäologisches Institut*, International Colloquium, Mainz: 79–94.

Perrot, J., 1985. 'Suse à la période achéménide',

Paléorient 11/ 2: 67–9.

Perrot, J., 1989. 'Shoshan ha-birah', *Eretz Israel* 20: 155–60.

Pillet, M., 1914. *Le palais de Darius Ier à Suse*, Paris.

Porada, E., 1965. *Ancient Iran*, London.

Postgate, J.N., and Reade, J.E., 1977–80. 'Kalhu', *Reallexikon der Assyriologie* V: 303–23.

Pritchard, J.B., 1955. *Ancient Near Eastern Texts relating to the Old Testament*, Princeton.

Pusey, E.B., 1892. *Daniel the Prophet. Nine Lectures*, London.

Ravn, O.E., 1942. *Herodotus' Description of Babylon*, Copenhagen.

Reade, J.E., 1986. 'A hoard of silver currency from Achaemenid Babylonia', *Iran* 24: 79–89.

Reiner, E., 1973. 'The Location of Anshan', *Revue d'Assyriologie* 67: 57–62.

Reuther, O., 1926. *Die Innenstadt von Babylon*, WVDO–G 47, Leipzig.

Roaf, M.D., 1974. 'The subject peoples on the base of the statue of Darius', *Cahiers de la Délégation Archéologique Française en Iran* 4: 73–160.

Roaf, M.D., 1983. *Sculptures and Sculptors at Persepolis*, Iran 21.

Roaf, M.D., 1995. 'Media and Mesopotamia: history and architecture', in Curtis, J.E. (ed.), *Later Mesopotamia and Iran*, London: 54–66.

Roberts, B.J., 1951. *The Old Testament Text and Versions*, Cardiff.

Robinson, E.S.G., 1950. 'A "silversmith's hoard" from Mesopotamia', *Iraq* 12: 44–51.

Rooker, M.F., 1990. *Biblical Hebrew in Transition. The Language of Ezekiel*, Sheffield.

Root, M.C., 1979. *The King and Kingship in Achaemenid Art*, Acta Iranica 19, Leiden.

Root, M.C., 1995. 'Art and archaeology of the Achaemenid empire', in Sasson, J.M. (ed.), *Civilizations of the Ancient Near East* IV, New York: 2615–37.

Rosenthal, F., 1974. *A Grammar of Biblical Aramaic*, Wiesbaden.

Roux, G., 1964. *Ancient Iraq*, London.

Rowley, H.H., 1935. *Darius the Mede and the Four World Empires in the Book of Daniel*, Cardiff.

Sachs, A.J., Pinches, T.G., and Strassmaier, J.N., 1955. *Late Babylonian Astronomical and Related Texts*, Brown University Studies 18, Providence, Rhode Island.

Sachs, A.J., and Hunger, H., 1988–1996. *Astronomical Diaries and Related Texts from Babylonia*, vols. I–III, Vienna.

Sancisi-Weerdenburg, H., 1995. 'Darius I and the Persian Empire', in Sasson, J.M. (ed.), *Civilizations of the Ancient Near East* II, New York: 1035–50.

Schmidt, E., 1941. 'Die Griechen in Babylon und das Weiterleben ihrer Kultur', *Archäologischer Anzeiger*: 786–844.

Schmitt, R., 1975. 'Altpersische Inschriften aus Babylon', *Die Sprache* 21/1: 42–3.

Seidl, U., 1976. 'Ein Relief Dareios I in Babylon', *Archaeologische Mitteilungen aus Iran,* new series 9: 125–30

Shaked, S., 1987. 'Iranian Loanwords in Middle Aramaic', *Encyclopaedia Iranica* II: 259–61.

Shea, W.H., 1971–72. 'An unrecognised vassal king of Babylon in the early Achaemenid period', *Andrews University Seminary Studies* 9: 51–67, 99–128; 10: 88–117, 147–78.

Shea, W.H., 1982. 'Darius the Mede: an update', *Andrews University Seminary Studies* 20: 229–47.

Simpson, St.J., 1990. 'Iron Age crop storage and ceramic manufacture in rural Mesopotamia: a review of the British Museum excavations at Qasrij Cliff and Khirbet Qasrij in Northern Iraq', *Institute of Archaeology Bulletin* 27: 119–40.

Simpson, St.J., 1995. 'Wider implications of the Achaemenid period ceramics', in Baird, D., *et al.* (eds) 1995: 142–6.

Sims-Williams, 1993. (Daniel) 'in Sogdian Literature', *Encyclopaedia Iranica* VI: 658.

Smith, S., 1944. *Isaiah Chapters XL–LV*, Schweich Lectures 1940, London.

Steele, J.M., forthcoming. 'Solar eclipse times predicted by the Babylonians', *Journal for the History of Astronomy*.

Stephenson, F. R., and Steele, J. M., forthcoming. 'Lunar eclipse times predicted by the Babylonians', *Journal for the History of Astronomy*.

Steve, M.J., 1974. 'Inscriptions des Achéménides à Suse (fouilles de 1952 à 1965)', *Studia Iranica* 3: 7–28.

Steve, M.J., 1987. *Nouveaux mélanges épigraphiques: Inscriptions royales de Suse et de la Susiane*, Mémoires de la Délégation Archéologique en Iran 53, Nice.

Stevenson, R.B., 1987. 'Lies and invention in Deinon's *Persica*', *Achaemenid History* 2: 27–35.

Stolper, M. W., 1985. *Entrepreneurs and Empire: the Murašû Archive, the Murašû Firm, and Persian Rule in Babylonia*, Leiden.

Stolper, M.W., 1989. 'The governor of Babylon and Across-the-River in 486 BC', *Journal of Near Eastern Studies* 48: 283–305.

Stolper, M.W., 1992. 'The Murašû texts from Susa', *Revue d'Assyriologie* 86: 69–77.

Stoops, G., Sr, & G., Jr., 1994. 'Petrographic study of red floor fragments from the palaces at Babylon and Susa', *Mesopotamian History and Environment. Occasional Publications* 2: 477–86.

Strassmaier, J.N., 1890. *Inschriften von Cambyses*, Leipzig.

Streck, M., 1934. 'Susan', *Encyclopaedia of Islam*

IV: 570–71.

Strommenger, E., 1964. 'Grabformen in Babylon', *Baghdader Mitteilungen* 3: 157–73.

Stronach, D.B., 1974a. 'La statue de Darius le Grand découverte à Suse', *Cahiers de la Délégation Archéologique Française en Iran* 4: 61–72.

Stronach, D.B., 1974b. 'Achaemenid Village I at Susa and the Persian Migration to Fars', *Iraq* 36: 239–48.

Stronach, D.B., 1978. *Pasargadae*, Oxford.

Stronach, D.B., and Roaf, M., 1978. 'Excavations at Tepe Nush-i Jan: Part I, a third interim report', *Iran* 16:1–11.

Stronach, D.B., 1985a. 'The Apadana: a signature of the line of Darius I', in Huot, J.-L., Yon, M., and Calvet, Y. (eds), *De l'Indus aux Balkans: Recueil à la mémoire de Jean Deshayes*, Paris: 433–45.

Stronach, D.B., 1985b. 'On the evolution of the early Iranian fire temple', *Acta Iranica* 25: 605–27.

Stronach, D.B., 1990. 'On the genesis of the Old Persian cuneiform script', in Vallat, F. (ed.), *Contribution à l'histoire de l'Iran: Mélanges Jean Perrot*, Paris: 195–203.

Stronach, D.B., 1994. 'Parterres and stone water-courses at Pasargadae: notes on the Achaemenid contribution to garden design', *Journal of Garden History* 14: 3–12.

Stronach, D.B, forthcoming, 'On the interpretation of the Pasargadae Inscriptions', *Carl Nylander Festschrift*.

Sumner, W.M., 1986. 'Achaemenid settlement in the Persepolis Plain', *American Journal of Archaeology* 90: 3–31.

Sumner, W. M., 1994. 'Archaeological measures of cultural continuity and the arrival of the Persians in Fars', *Achaemenid History* VIII: 97–105.

Swete, H.B., 1930. *The Old Testament in Greek According to the Septuagint* III, Cambridge.

Tekriti, A. Q., al-, 1960. 'The excavations at Tell ed-Daim (Dokan)', *Sumer* 16: 93–109 (in Arabic).

Toomer, G.J., 1984. *Ptolemy's Almagest*, London.

Ulrich, E., 1987. 'Daniel Manuscripts from Qumran. Part I: A Preliminary Edition of 4QDanᵃ', *Bulletin of the American Schools of Oriental Research* 268: 17–37.

Ulrich, E., 1989. 'Daniel Manuscripts from Qumran. Part 2: Preliminary Editions of 4QDanᵇ and 4QDanᶜ', *Bulletin of the American Schools of Oriental Research* 274: 3–26.

Vallat, F., 1970. 'Table élamite de Darius Ier', *Revue d'Assyriologie* 64: 149–60.

Vallat, F., 1974. 'Les textes cunéiformes de la statue de Darius', and 'L'inscription trilingue de Xerxès à la Porte de Darius', *Cahiers de la Délégation Archéologique Française en Iran* 4: 161–83.

Vallat, F., 1979. 'Les inscriptions du palais d'Artaxerxès II', *Cahiers de la Délégation Archéologique Française en Iran* 10: 145–9.

Vallat, F., 1986. 'Table accadienne de Darius Ier (DSaa)', in De Meyer, L., Gasche, H., and Vallat, F. (eds), *Fragmenta Historiae Elamicae: Mélanges offerts à M.J. Steve*, Paris: 277–87.

Vallat, F., 1989. 'Le palais d'Artaxerxès II à Babylone', *Northern Akkad Project Reports* 2: 3–6.

Vallat, F., 1995. 'Susa and Susiana in Second-Millennium Iran', in Sasson, J.M. (ed.), *Civilizations of the Ancient Near East* II: 1023–33.

Walker, C.B.F., and Britton, J., 1996. 'Astronomy and astrology in Mesopotamia', in Walker, C.B.F. (ed.), *Astronomy before the Telescope*, London: 42–67.

Wenke, R.J., 1975-76. 'Imperial investments and agricultural developments in Parthian and Sasanian Khuzestan: 150 BC to AD 640', *Mesopotamia* 10–11: 31–221.

Wetzel, F., 1931. 'Der Perserbau im Westen der Südburg', *Mitteilungen der Deutschen Orient-Gesellschaft* 69: 14–16.

Wetzel, F., 1944. 'Babylon zur Zeit Herodots', *Zeitschrift für Assyriologie* 48: 45–68.

Wetzel, F., 1950. 'Babylon bei den klassischen Schriftstellern ausser Herodot', *Mitteilungen der Deutschen Orient-Gesellschaft* 82: 47–53.

Wetzel, F., Schmidt, E., and Mallwitz, A., 1957. *Das Babylon der Spätzeit*, WVDO-G 62, Berlin.

Wiggerman, F.A.M., 1992. *Mesopotamian Protective Spirits: The Ritual Texts*, Groningen.

Wilber, D.N., 1969. *Persepolis*, London.

Wiseman, D.J., 1965. 'Some historical problems in the Book of Daniel', in Wiseman, D.J., *et al.*, *Notes on Some Problems in the Book of Daniel*, London: 9–18.

Woolley, C.L., 1938. 'The excavations at al Mina, Sueidia, II', *Journal of Hellenistic Studies* LVIII: 133–70.

Wurthwein, E., 1979. *The Text of the Old Testament*, London.

Young, E.J., 1949. *The Prophecy of Daniel*, Grand Rapids.

Young, T. C. and Levine, L.D., 1974. *Excavations of the Godin Project: Second Progress Report*, Toronto.

Zadok, R., 1976. 'On the connections between Iran and Babylonia in the sixth century BC', *Iran* 14: 61–78.

Zadok, R., 1991. 'Elamite Onomastics', *Studi Epigrafici e Linguistici* 8: 225–37.

Zadok, R., 1995. 'On the current state of Elamite lexicography', *Studi Epipigrafici e Linguistici* 12: 241–52.

Zettler, R., 1979. 'On the chronological range of Neo-Babylonian and Achaemenid seals', *Journal of Near Eastern Studies* 38: 257–70.

Illustration Acknowledgements

BM = Photograph by courtesy of the Trustees of the British Museum

Figures

1 Photo BM.

2 Photo J. E. Curtis.

3 Photo J. E. Curtis.

4 Photo BM.

5 Map by Ann Searight.

6-7 BM 32234.

8 From Koldewey 1931: pl. 28.

9 From Schmidt 1941: figs 10–11.

10 From Koldewey 1931: pl. 7.

11 From Boehmer 1973: fig. 21.

12 From Legrain 1925: figs 891, 905, 910, 913, 922, 925, 951–5, 983–4.

13 From von Gall 1988: figs. 4, 6.

14 Drawing by Eleanor Barbanes, University of California, Berkeley.

15 From Garrison 1991: fig. 2 (with thanks to M. B. Garrison, M. C. Root and the Oriental Institute for permission to publish).

16 From Alizadeh 1985: fig. 4.

17 From Stronach 1978: fig. 25.

18 From Stronach 1978: fig. 34.

19 From Layard 1853: fig. on p. 462.

20 From Porada 1965: fig. 15.

21 From Stronach 1994: fig. 1.

22 After Amiet 1988: fig. 3.

23 From Perrot 1989: fig. III.5.

24 From Perrot 1989: fig. III.4.

25 From Stronach 1974a: fig. 20.

26 From Boucharlat and Labrousse 1979: fig. 6.

27 From Loftus 1857: facing p. 322.

28–30 T. C. Mitchell.

Black and white plates

1 BM 124017.

2 BM 89132.

3 BM 1994–1–27, 1.

4 Photo BM.

5 From Koldewey 1931: pl. 39.

6 From Wetzel *et al.* 1957: pl. 25a–b.

7 From Otto 1944: fig. 5a.

8 BM 120450.

9 From Hrouda 1962: pl. 17, no. 137.

10 From Hrouda 1962: pl. 17, no. 141.

11 BM 90920.

12 Photo Pasargadae expedition.

13 From Stronach 1978: pl. 188.

14 From Stronach 1978: pl. 59.

15 From Harper *et al.* 1992: no. 142.

16 From Kambaksh Fard 1995: fig. on pp 380–1.

17 From Stronach 1978: pl. 189d.

18 From Stronach 1978: pl. 189c.

19 From Stronach 1978: pl. 90a.

20 Photo BM.

13 Photo R. Boucharlat.

22 From Amiet 1988: fig. 79.

23 Photo R. Boucharlat.

Colour Plates

I Photo J. E. Curtis.

II BM 118838.

III Photo J. E. Curtis.

IV Photo D. B. Stronach.

V Photo Pasargadae expedition.

VI Photo Pasargadae expedition.

VII Photo Pasargadae expedition.

VIII Photo Pasargadae expedition.

IX Photo Pasargadae expedition.

X Photo Pasargadae expedition.

XI Collection of Mme Pillet, Le Chesnay, France, reproduced by permission of the Départment des Antiquités Orientales, Musée du Louvre.

XII Collection of Mme Pillet, Le Chesnay, France, reproduced by permission of the Départment des Antiquités Orientales, Musée du Louvre.

XIII BM 132525.

XIV–XV Photo R. Boucharlat.

XVI Photo R. Boucharlat.

XVII From de Morgan 1905: pl. II.

1 Gold bracelet from the Oxus Treasure.

2 Cylinder seal with inscription of Darius showing a royal lion hunt.

PLATES

3 Silver bowl with inscription of Artaxerxes.

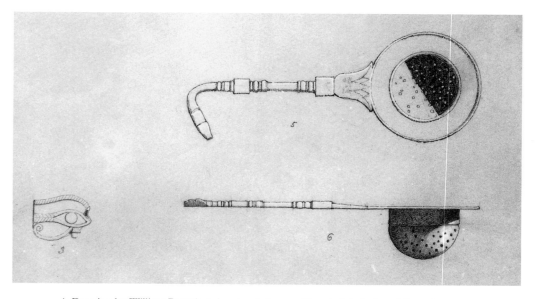

4 Drawing by William Boutcher showing Achaemenid period finds from Nimrud.

5 Glazed brick from the small palace at Babylon

6 *Below* Column bases at Abu Chulfat

7 *Above* Gold bracelet from Nippur

8 *Right* Silver jar handle from a hoard found at Babylon

9 *Below* Terracotta horse-and-rider figurine from Tell Halaf

10 Terracotta figurine from Tell Halaf showing a woman riding in a pannier mounted on a horse.

11 The 'Cyrus Cylinder'. The one document, owed to Cyrus the Great, which provides a record of his genealogy.

12 Pasargadae. The tomb of Cyrus, photographed in 1961.

13 Khorsabad. Winged genius from the palace of Sargon II of Assyria, *c.*710–705 BC.

14 Palace S, Pasargadae. Detail of a partly restored doorway relief showing the extant remains of the finely carved 'fish-garbed man'. The legs of the associated bull-man, and the lower part of the staff of the latter's tall standard, are also visible.

15 Limestone apotropaic plaque from Neo-Elamite Susa.

16 Bisitun. Detail of the representation of Ahuramazda. The deep, circular incision adjacent to the god's left hand presumably once held an inset gold ring.

17 *Above left* Bisitun. Detail of the robes of Darius and Gaumata.

18 *Above right* Bisitun. Head of Darius the Great.

19 Pasargadae. A square stone basin from one of the water-courses of the Royal Garden.

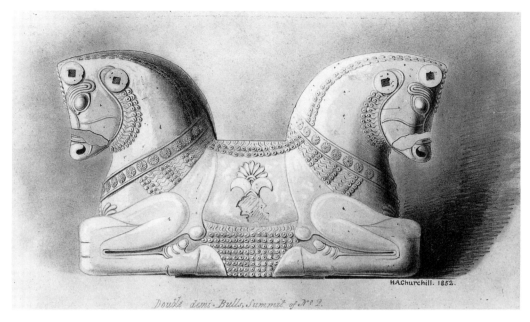

Double demi-Bulls, Summit of N° 2.

H.A.Churchill. 1852.

20 Drawing by H.A. Churchill of column capital in form of double bull protome from the Apadana at Susa.

21 Base of the statue of Darius found at Susa in 1972.

22 A reconstructed column with its capital from the Apadana of Darius at Susa.

23 The hypostyle hall in the Palace of Artaxerxes II near the Shaur river at Susa.

I Fallen columns from the Palace of Darius at Susa.

II Palace S at Pasargadae.

III Row of four Persian guardsmen from the Apadana at Persepolis.

IV Detail from the left side of the rock relief of Darius at Bisitun. Darius, followed by his bow bearer and spear bearer, places his leading foot on the pleading, prostrate form of Gaumata. His raised right hand, palm forwards, salutes the elevated image of Ahuramazda (part of which can be seen hovering above the first three of the nine roped 'captive kings').

v Pasargadae. The denuded eight-columned hall of Gate R from the north-west. The door jamb bearing the relief of the winged figure stands at the mid-point of the hall's long north-east wall.

VI Palace P, Pasargadae. The north-east elevation of the inscribed anta, showing the trilingual CMa inscription in Old Persian, Elamite and Akkadian.

VII Palace P, Pasargadae. The right hand jamb of the north-west doorway showing the surviving portion of a representation of Cyrus, carved and inscribed early in the reign of Darius. Note also the provision for gold insets on the hem and on the vertical pleats of the king's robe.

VIII A view of the excavations at Pavilion B towards the end of the 1963 season. The Pasargadae Treasure was found, three days from the close of the season, directly beside the wall of the portico in the right foreground.

X *Below* The Pasargadae Treasure: a gold penannular earring with a large gold and lapis lazuli pendant at the base. The wire mesh tube that forms the perimeter of the earring illustrates an advanced goldworking technique that was first introduced during the 4th century BC.

IX The Pasargadae Treasure: a gold bracelet with a spirally twisted wire hoop and ibex-headed terminals.

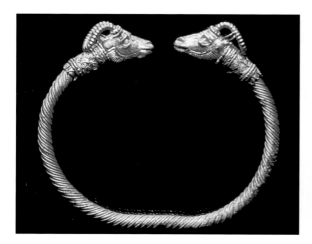

XI Watercolour by Maurice Pillet, 1913, showing the columns of the Apadana at Susa and the chateau in the background.

XII Watercolour by Maurice Pillet, 1913, showing his hypothetical reconstruction of the Palace of Darius at Susa.

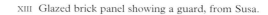
XIII Glazed brick panel showing a guard, from Susa.

XIV–XV Two fragments of wall paintings in the Shaur Palace at Susa depicting 'peoples' of the empire.

XVI An orthostat from the Shaur Palace at Susa showing a servant climbing a stair.

XVII Watercolour showing the Achaemenid burial at Susa.

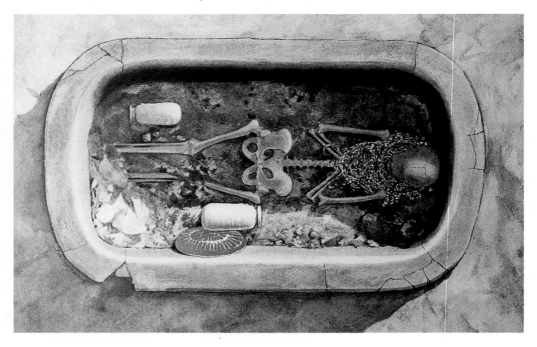